BRGC1

ORCHIDS for
Home and Garden

ORCHIDS for Home and Garden

Revised Edition

by T. A. FENNELL, JR.

DRAWINGS BY THE AUTHOR

Rinehart & Company, Inc.

New York   Toronto

Published simultaneously in Canada by
Clarke, Irwin & Company, Ltd., Toronto

Library of Congress Catalog Card Number: 59–11789

Acknowledgments

First Edition

Many friends deserve my thanks for their generously shared time, experience and advice in helping me produce this book. I would like to express my most heartfelt appreciation to: Mr. and Mrs. Philip Wylie and Mr. and Mrs. Stanley M. Rinehart, Jr. for their constant encouragement and unfailing interest; to my mother and my wife without whose encouragements and gentle proddings the book would never have been finished. Most of all my thanks are due to T. A. Fennell, Sr., my father, from whom I have learned most of what I know about orchids; thanks to him also for the time and the background which made possible the writing of this book and for his ever-fresh approach to everything—including books and orchids. He has been my inspiration and my mentor.

Second Edition

In the three years since the first edition of this book was published, several major advances in the methods of orchid culture have occurred. These new discoveries make the hobby of growing orchids at home even easier; more fun and less work! I have tried to cover these new topics fully for the benefit of the beginner and hobby-grower of orchids. In addition, I have included several new features suggested by friends and asked for by readers of the first edition.

The response to the first edition was tremendously gratifying to me, and I hope that this revised edition will prove even more helpful and useful to those who want to learn about orchids and how to grow them. The Orchid Family is a fascinating group of plants; the Orchid Hobby is a rewarding one—both in beauty and creative achievement! Orchids for Pleasant Living—for Gracious Giving!

A Personal Preamble

For a good many years, the ladies in my immediate family, not only here in South Florida but in Baltimore and the Buffalo area, have been able on frequent occasions to adorn themselves with spectacular orchids—almost without cost. That is to say, they have raised the plants from low-priced young specimens to glamorous maturity at home—outdoors in Florida, in bay windows or on a south-facing sill up North. They spent less time and trouble on the enterprise than they'd previously devoted to many familiar house plants. They used no fancy equipment—no mist sprays, pumps to humidify the air, glass maisonettes, or other gadgets—items which, until quite recently, were presumed essential for indoor orchid culture above the subtropic zone.

Here in South Florida they just went out in the yard and picked big *Cattleyas*—the kind that florists most commonly sell at prices that appall young men. They picked these fabled blooms from plants that grew on my live oak trees exactly as they (or their ancestors) once grew in forests and glades on Central and South American mountainsides—or in the Philippines, or Malaya, or even more bizarre and distant places. They picked almost pure white *Cattleyas*—year after year, and white ones with yellow centers, mauve, or chartreuse, or raspberry—and great lavender orchids nine inches across—as well as moth orchids, spray orchids and. . . . But such detail is the concern of the book ahead!

By that phenomenon I was, am, and expect to remain—stunned. I have always liked flowers. I am fond of gardening. My parents were fairly "advanced" vegetable and rose raisers in the Midwest. But it did not occur to me that handiness with hoe, cultivator, pruning knife and spray gun could lead to orchids. Indeed, during my early manhood, that great family of flowers was merely a dream, beyond my experience and my purse. I was the sort who sent a bunch of violets to my date—or, on great occasions, a gardenia or two.

How, then, the transition?

It began with a tenth wedding anniversary. Like many loving husbands facing that quandary, I searched an almanac for the appropriate gift. "Wooden objects" it said—so I bought a set of wooden salad bowls. But the almanac had also said "orchids." And on the way home from the gift shop I passed a flower shop. There was to be a party that night for Mrs. Wylie and me, celebrating ten happy years in marriage; so she would wear orchids, I thought. But when the florist showed me his gaudy wares some impulse made me ask, "Is it possible to buy an orchid *plant* bearing flowers like that—and to keep the plant until it blooms again? Or do they just die?"

The florist was dubious. They had a greenhouse. In it were hundreds of orchid plants. Perhaps the head gardener would sell a plant. It would be expensive. Some people in the area did manage to re-bloom a few plants. The florist gave me the impression, however, that such people were horticultural geniuses, touched with luck besides.

Now, I am not merely a man of impulse, but, unlike most such people, I am exceedingly stubborn about my impulses. I drove to the greenhouse.

The plant I bought was a *hybrid Cattleya*—but I then knew neither of those terms. It was pale lavender, with a fringed lip (indicating a *Brasso-cattleya* cross), but I didn't even know they called that part of the flower a "lip." The greenhouse man dubiously told me how to water and sun the awkward-looking, leather-leafed herb —on which, at the moment, were half a dozen magnificent blooms. My wife was delighted. She cut off three flowers that evening and wore them to the party.

The plant survived, moreover. A year later, it bloomed again. A few months after that, its pot was accidentally smashed, but we re-potted it (after inquiry) and, again, it bloomed. Then we built a new house in a part of South Florida which was unincorporated jungle. We heard that such orchids as ours, if wired to a tree, would grow fast to it, and not hurt the tree, since orchids aren't parasites. We wired it to a live oak. It bloomed a third time. After that, we moved it again—to some oaks behind the house: it didn't miss its annual beat.

By that time, we were convinced that the orchid—or, at least, the *Cattleya*, which is the showiest member of the family—is a remarkably hardy plant. And at about that time we noticed, on local highways, signs directing us to an "Orchid Jungle" some miles south of us. In due course, we followed the signs and made the acquaintance of the charming parents of the author of this book, Dorothy and Tom Fennell.

Thomas Fennell, Senior, in those days, was carrying on a not large orchid retailing and hybridizing business which had been established by his father almost seventy years ago and is, in consequence, one of the oldest orchid companies of the kind in America. But there was, and had always been, one difference between the Fennell Orchid Company of Homestead, Florida, and all others:

The *grandfather* of the author of this book, coming to South Florida long ago, had tried an experiment. He purchased a twenty-five-acre jungle "hammock." A "hammock" is an islandlike rise of land above the low-lying Everglades or the flat, peninsular parts of Florida. It is usually covered with hardwoods, with Caribbean trees and shrubs, and a tangle of thorny vines. The eldest Fennell undertook to naturalize in this region varied orchids that grew wild in upland parts of more tropical countries. The result, when Mrs. Wylie and I first saw it years ago, was a natural orchid garden in a whelming, dark, West Indian type of jungle. Among the live oaks, tamarinds, gumbo limbos, push-and-haul vines, wild coffee bushes, air plants and zebra butterflies—exotic orchids, which one usually associates with either Yucatán or Fifth Avenue florists, glowed in the gloom like massed blowtorches.

And—a point that interested Mrs. Wylie but really gripped me —some of the most magnificent specimens, with hundreds of blooms, had lived on the same tree branches *for a quarter of a century without any care whatever!* No spraying. No fertilizing. No humidifying. No protection from the cold spells. Nothing.

Now, I am a gardener who—within reason, and if time permits —is willing to play nursemaid to special plants for adequate floral rewards. But I am also one who greatly prefers a plant, shrub, vine or tree which, once established, can be relied on to fend for itself—

come deluge or drought, hurricane, insects in armadas, what not.

The fact that Grandpa Fennell's orchids—stupendous sorts of orchids—could grow and *had* grown untended for all those years right in South Florida, appealed prodigiously to me. I asked Mr. Tom Fennell, Sr. to furnish my wife and myself with a plant or two of the kind blazing in the green labyrinth of his "Orchid Jungle."

The next day Mr. Fennell brought the plants to our house. They were fixed to our trees with wire lead around limbs and over chunks of osmunda (a kind of fern root) which was used to retain for a time any water that reached the roots. More than five years later, those plants are still on the same limbs.

Our success with this initial, minute collection led us to experiment further. We learned how to use the hydroponic fertilizer, which the Fennell family had invented and perfected for orchids—in the face of a widespread notion among amateur and professional orchid growers that there was no way to "feed" such plants. We also learned from the Fennells their simple and equally original "cake tin" method of growing orchids indoors, up North. It is another procedure which they perfected in the face of a long tradition that insisted the Northern indoor plantsmen needed special heating equipment, humidifiers and other very costly impedimenta to bloom a single *Cattleya*.

Mrs. Wylie's mother, the late Mrs. Jennie O. Ballard, of Rushford, New York, was as fond of house plants—and all plants—as her daughter. She was a good hand with gloxinia and African violets. So we sent her a Fennell orchid plant. It throve through one of the coldest winters in the Buffalo area—on an ordinary, steam-heated sun porch—and rebloomed. In the following years, Mrs. Ballard maintained moth orchids (*Phalaenopsis*) in full bloom for a hundred days and successfully rebloomed other species, many times. So did and does my wife's sister, Mrs. John Cosgrove, who lives even farther north!

As my own collection increased slowly and my Northern in-laws astounded friends, I wrote in *The Saturday Evening Post* and in *Reader's Digest* about this "new house plant" which the ingenuity of the Fennell family had made practicable everywhere. Others, far more competent—gardening editors and the like—tried the experiment, verified it and described it in other magazines.

Tom Senior had sent his sons to Harvard. One studied medicine. The other, who wrote this volume, started to train for a diplomatic career. But something about orchids, the Florida "jungles," the flower business, made him change over to botany. Tom Junior graduated from Harvard, returned to Homestead, and is now, with his mother and his wife Trudy, a partner in the company. He has become one of the authorities on orchids—on their taxonomy, breeding, cultivation, maintenance in alien climes, fertilization, shipment, insect control, and on other orchid-related and highly complex matters.

Over the same period, the Fennell Orchid Company of Homestead—or "Orchid Jungle" as it is known in the Miami areas—has grown from its modest circumstances into the largest retail orchid-plant business in the world. Moreover, owing to the numbers of thriving competitors in South Florida, Miami—not Hawaii, not Costa Rica nor Malaga—is now the "orchid capital" of the world, with the world's greatest annual orchid show!

All I'm *trying* to say is that raising orchids is a beautiful kind of fun, anyplace, and the author of this book tells you about it lucidly, completely and with tested, up-to-date, information for the layman, amateur, beginner and others about the world's most fabulous plant family.

Read it . . . and then. . . .

Well, read it. Even *that's* fun!

PHILIP WYLIE

South Miami, Florida
Friday, January 13, 1956

Contents

ORCHIDS for
Home and Garden

chapter 1

Orchids As House Plants

You can grow orchids in your home. You need only a sunny window and a few minutes a week.

You may doubt this—most people do at first—but thousands already are doing it, and everyday more are finding out how easily it can be done. Growing orchids in the home is one of the most rapidly increasing indoor hobbies of recent years. From Maine to California, from Alaska to South Africa, interest increases by leaps and bounds as people begin to realize that many kinds of orchids actually thrive in the home.

Orchids will grow and bloom better with less work than most of the more commonly known house plants. Their wants are simple and few. You can almost say that they like the same living conditions as human beings! They are either already present in the average home or easily supplied for the plants.

WARMTH   Orchids like the same temperatures that you do—*the average home temperatures from 60° to 80° F. are ideal for them.* They can stand short drops down to freezing and rises up to 120° F. without any serious damage, but normally should be kept in the 60° to 80° F. range.

Orchids are different from other plants in some respects. Most important is the fact that the more commonly grown types of orchids are epiphytes or "air plants" as they are usually called. In the wild, these orchids grow in an elevated position either on trees or cliffs. In such a position they have very good ventilation, and this is important to their growth.

AIR-VENTILATION   *Orchids like a fresh-feeling atmosphere that is neither stuffy nor excessively muggy.*

Probably the most important and different thing about the culture of orchids is that they have a special type of root which must dry out thoroughly between waterings. These roots run out over the surface of the tree or cliff on which the plant grows, and they are exposed to the air at all times. When it rains, the roots get completely wet, and as soon as it stops raining, the breezes blow, and the roots dry out.

Putting orchid roots in a pot creates an artificial condition, and if you are not careful, it will be easy to keep them too wet. If they are kept constantly wet for very long, they will rot. In order to allow the roots to dry out quickly after they are watered, we pot orchids in osmunda fiber (the roots of a fern), or small chunks of tree bark (pine or fir), which are quite coarse and therefore allow both good drainage and ventilation. For the same reasons—drainage and ventilation—most orchids are grown in pots which have several slits cut into the sides.

WATER *Orchids like a lot of water, but they must be allowed to become bone dry between waterings.* When you water, water heavily —two or three quarts to the average pot—and don't water again until the fiber or bark is bone dry all the way through the pot. It is easy to tell when the pot is really dry all the way through by touching it. If it feels clammy or damp and cooler than air temperature, water is still evaporating from it. If the pot feels dry and at room temperature, you can be sure that it is fairly dry all the way through.

Don't try to set up a definite time schedule for watering. No two pots require watering on the same schedule. Small pots will dry out more quickly than larger ones. Speed of drying also depends on the potting material used, the size of the particles or coarseness of the fiber and how tightly they are packed into the pot. In general plants potted in bark will need water more often than ones in osmunda.

This matter of watering is without a doubt the hardest part of orchid culture for the beginner to learn, and, unfortunately, it is the most important. If you must err, err on the side of too little water rather than too much.

FOOD Like you and any other living organism, orchids must be fed. Also like humans they prefer their food regularly. A special orchid fertilizer designed to fit their needs is best for them. Most of these fertilizers are hydroponic plant foods—ones that can be dissolved in water and given to the plant just like a regular watering. The Fennell Orchid Company of Homestead, Florida, manufactures such a fertilizer especially for orchids. *This fertilizer should be dissolved in water and given to the plants every other time they are watered.* In the past orchids have been grown without any special fertilizer, but it has been found in recent years that much larger and stronger plants and many more flowers are the result of a regular feeding schedule.

Plants potted in fir bark need much more nitrogen than do plants in osmunda. The bark supplies almost no nitrogen to the plants and a special type of fungus grows on the wood fiber in the bark and steals much of the nitrogen you feed the plants. This fungus does not attack the orchid but it must be fed nitrogen in large amounts so that some is left over for the orchid. If regular orchid food is used, then it should be supplemented with in-between feedings of Ammonium nitrate, on an alternate schedule.

In the last 2 or 3 years several new foods have been developed especially for orchids in fir bark. These are quite high in food analysis —as much as 30-10-10 and 20-20-20. (These figures refer to percentages of primary ingredients: Nitrogen, Phosphate and Potassium.) Such high-strength foods must be used carefully or roots may be burned. The safest way to feed is to use the regular orchid food and supplement with in-between feedings of Ammonium nitrate, at the rate of one teaspoonful to a gallon of water. This gives the plant a well-balanced diet and will not burn.

Feeding plants potted in *PINE BARK* is different too. Pine Bark supplies a considerable amount of food to the plants but in an unbalanced ratio. Therefore the feeding program must be planned to adjust the ratio properly for best plant growth. Pine Bark supplies just about enough Phosphate for good growth and considerably more Potassium than is necessary. However, it is extremely low in Nitrogen and somewhat low on the micro-nutrients or trace-elements as they are sometimes called. (These are chemicals known to be needed for proper plant growth but only in very minute quantities—a few parts per million.) Therefore heavy feeding with nitrogen is also necessary in Pine Bark and very little other food is required. A specially balanced food for orchids growing in Pine Bark is now being developed by The Fennell Orchid Company and it will soon be available. In

1.   ORCHID PLANTS GROWING IN A SOUTH WINDOW.

the meantime, weekly feedings with Ammonium nitrate, at the rate of one teaspoonful to a gallon of water will do nicely.

SUN   Orchids, like all green plants, need sun in order to grow and bloom well. Many house plants can get along without actual sun for long periods of time, but even these will not do well without some actual sunlight. Orchids, like philodendron, will grow but will not bloom without sun.

For best results orchids want lots of sunlight. They will take even more than most orchid growers realize. In the wild, orchids grow on tree trunks and in the tops of trees where they get quite a bit of sun. They are almost never found growing in dark, jungly places. Usually they are found either in open woods or on isolated trees in open fields. Ideally speaking, they would like full sun in the morning up until about ten thirty, half sun from ten thirty until three p.m., and full sun for the rest of the afternoon. Naturally this is hard to give them, and a compromise of one-half sun and one-half shade all day long is sufficient.

In the Northern United States the winter sun is not nearly as intense as the tropical sun that the orchids are used to. Therefore, *during the winter months from November to March, the plants should be in a south window where they will get as much sun as possible.* East or west windows that get at least two or three hours of sun a day can also be used, but a south window is best. *From April through October the sun is nearly as intense as the tropical sun, so some shade will be needed during the middle of the day at least.* Window screens usually give sufficient shade to keep the plants from burning. Light gauze or lace curtains across the window in front of the plants will also give them plenty of shade. If you prefer, the plants can be moved to an east window where they get only the morning sun during the summer months, which will be enough if they get it all morning long. A west window can be used too if the plants have about one-half shade in the early afternoon.

In the Southern United States, where the sun is more intense, some shade is necessary during the middle of the day even through the winter months. The most important thing to learn is that the more sun the plants get, the more flowers you will get, *but* it is possible to burn plants by giving them full sun during the middle of the day when the sun is intense.

Sunburns on orchid leaves are easy to recognize. Within twenty-four hours after the plant has been exposed to too much sun, large areas of the leaf, often the size of a fifty-cent piece, will start to turn brown or black with a gray-white edge. (*See* Fig. 21.) This area is usually sunk below the level of the rest of the leaf. These spots can be cut out of the leaves for the sake of the appearance of the plant, but actually nothing need be done to them as they will soon dry up and become merely unsightly but not dangerous scars.

ARTIFICIAL LIGHT   If you simply don't have enough natural sunlight for your orchids you can use artificial light to supplement the sun. You can even grow orchids under artificial light entirely if you are willing to build the proper setup to supply the necessary light intensity.

To supplement sun in a window Fluorescent tubes of the Deluxe Cool White types are best. These can be mounted just above the plants in home-built reflector boxes that fit across the window, as shown in the photo of Mr. and Mrs. Ted Leitzell in the illustrated section following page 18. These tubes also can be mounted in standard commercial reflectors at either side of the window behind your draperies. In this case, the tubes would run vertically and the reflectors should be angled to throw the most light directly onto the plants.

In either case, the lights should be as close to the leaves as possible as the intensity of light decreases very rapidly with additional distance between lights and leaves.

These "growing" lights should be used only during daylight hours. Use at night may result in a change of the blooming season or may prohibit blooming entirely.

In Chapter 10, "Orchids Under Artificial Light," the use of artificial light is discussed more fully, with directions for the proper setups to supply sufficient intensities for good plant growth and flowering.

SUN-FOOD RATIO   The amounts of food and sunlight which your plants need are closely related to each other. The more sun your plant gets, the more food it needs and vice versa. It is easy to tell if orchid plants are getting sun and food in the correct ratio by the color of the plant and the way in which it is growing.

Orchid plants that are getting enough food and enough sun will be a clear grass-green in color, and they will be heavy, stocky plants with relatively straight leaves. Plants that are not getting enough sun will be tall, slender plants with twisted leaves and a dark velvety-green color. (Although these plants are pretty, they will not bloom well.)

If the new growths on your plants come out horizontally from the pot towards the window, instead of upright as is normal, this, too, is a sign of lack of sun. These growths are usually quite weak, spindly and drooping, and seldom bloom. Try to find a sunnier window for such plants, or give them more light with fluorescent tubes as described earlier. The resultant growth should again be normal.

Plants that are not getting enough food will be a yellowish green color and skinny or thin.

2. ORCHID PLANTS ON A TEA WAGON This can be moved easily from window to window following the sun, a practical labor saver when no one window supplies suitable conditions of sun. It can also be moved back from the window at night to avoid cold drafts. Notice that a tin pan has been made, covering the entire top of the wagon. This is for humidity, like the "Cake Pan" method described on the next page.

HUMIDITY   *Orchids need considerably more humidity than is
normally present in the heated home.* Average home humidity is 10
to 15 per cent. Orchids like 50 to 70 per cent relative humidity.
Actually the lack of humidity is the main problem in growing house
plants of any sort. Luckily, humidity is easily supplied.

Equipment is simple and cheap. You need only:

1. A large cake pan, Pyrex baking dish, or other shallow and
    wide container that will hold water
2. Gravel, or aquarium shells
3. Water

Place the dish or pan on the window sill or on a table in front of
the window where the plants will get the sun that they need. Fill
the pan with gravel or aquarium shells and keep it about one half to
two thirds full of water. Then place the plant in its pot on the gravel
so that it is sitting **above** the water, not in it. As the water evapo-
rates, the moisture comes up around the plant so that it sits in a
constant updraft of humidity. This evaporation is not enough to
change the humidity in the room as a whole to any great extent, but
it is sufficient for good growing conditions. The kitchen and the
bathroom are the most humid rooms in your home. For this reason,
if they have sunny windows, they are the best rooms for growing
orchids.

There are on the market several expensive indoor greenhouses
(table models) and orchid cases or Wardian cases, as they are often
called, designed to supply and retain humidity for orchid plants.
These are recommended by some people, but the author has found
that actually they are more likely to be a hindrance than a help as all
too often they supply 100 per cent humidity, which is far worse than
not enough. The Cake Pan Method explained above is an all-around
better way to grow orchids and much less expensive as well. Thousands of people are using this method with excellent results. The
Fennell Orchid Company has been advising this method for twelve
years, and they now have thousands of customers in every state of
the United States, every province of Canada, and several in Alaska
using this method successfully to grow their orchids.

If your home is exceptionally dry and the cake-pan method does
not supply quite enough humidity after a fair trial, then an easy way

to hold more humidity around the plants is with polyethylene bags, such as the laundry uses to pack your blankets after cleaning. These bags can be draped down over the whole plant with the bottom left

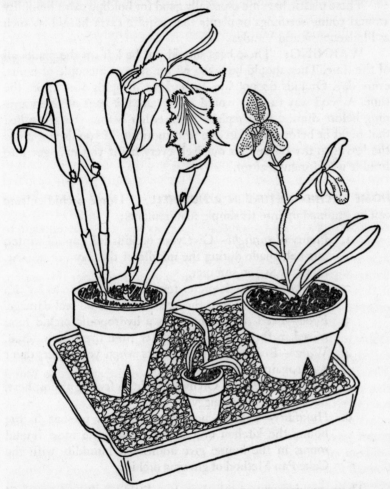

3. THE FENNELL "CAKE PAN" METHOD OF GROWING ORCHIDS used to supply the needed humidity for orchids in the home, described under the heading of Humidity. Note that the plants sit on the gravel with the bottom of the pot ABOVE the water level. Plant at left is *Bc. Diadem*, right is *Cypripedium Concolor*, center is a *Cattleya* seedling.

hanging open at about the level of the top of the pot. These polyethylene bags allow air to pass through them but will not allow water
vapor to escape.

These plastic bags are especially good for holding extra humidity
around young seedlings or plants that require extra humidity, such
as Phalaenopsis and Vandas.

WARNING: These bags should not be left on the plants all
of the time. They should be taken off for at least a couple of hours,
every day. Orchids do not like to be kept dripping wet all of the
time. A good way to do it would be to take the bags off every evening before dinner, then replace them either before you go to bed
that night or before breakfast the next morning. If you do not allow
the leaves to dry off and air out well every night you may get into
trouble with fungus leaf-rot.

HOME ORCHID CULTURE IN A NUTSHELL   Home orchid culture
can be summed up into six simple requirements:

1. *Plenty of sunlight*—Give your orchids full sun all winter,
    one-half shade during the middle of the day (10:30 A.M.
    to 3:00 P.M.) in summer.
2. *Warmth*—Orchids prefer temperatures of 60° to 80° F.;
    short drops even into the 30's will cause no real damage.
3. *Food*—Feed your plants with a hydroponic orchid food
    mixed in their water every other time they are watered.
4. *Water*—Really soak your plants when you water; don't
    water again until bone dry.
5. *Air or ventilation*—Orchids like fresh-feeling atmosphere,
    neither stuffy nor muggy.
6. *Humidity*—Orchids need more than is present in the
    home; the kitchen and bathroom are the most humid
    rooms in the house; give additional humidity with the
    Cake Pan Method of growing orchids.

These requirements applied with a little common sense will
give you success with your orchids. When in doubt, remember that
they like about the same conditions for living that you do.

chapter 2

Orchids in the Garden

DURING THE SUMMER MONTHS IN THE NORTH You can grow your orchids outdoors in the garden whenever there is no danger of freezing weather, and actually, the plants will do even better outdoors than they will indoors as, after all, outdoor conditions are natural for them. The growing requirements for orchids outdoors are essentially the same as their indoor requirements, but in most respects they are much easier to give to the plants out of doors.

In the North plants may be grown outside from May or June after the danger of cold weather is past until early in the fall, when frost danger is likely to start. Those of you who are lucky enough to live in the South can grow your orchids out of doors for longer periods of time. And if you happen to be far enough South so that you seldom or never have actual freezing temperatures, the orchids can be grown out of doors the year round.

Most orchids are not at all sensitive to sudden changes in temperatures. They can stand temperatures even below freezing for an hour or two, and they can stand temperatures well above 100° F. for short periods of time. In the wild, most orchid plants grow in mountainous country where they are constantly subjected to rapid temperature changes, and many orchids even get occasional frosts and freezes in their natural homes. When you get up three thousand to seven thousand feet in the mountains even in the tropics, you do have occasional cold weather.

TEMPERATURES *Most orchid plants prefer temperatures in the 60° to 80° F. range, however, and it is not advisable to put them outdoors until your temperatures are likely to stay somewhere within this range most of the time at least.*

FOOD   Orchid plants growing in pots will need their fertilizer whether they are indoors or out and *should be fertilized just as frequently when they are outdoors as when they are inside—every other time they are watered.*

SUN   The most important part of taking care of your plants out of doors is finding the correct location for growing them where they will get the right amounts of sun and shade. Remember that the summer sun even in the North is almost as intense as the tropical sun so that the plants must be shaded somewhat during the middle part of the day at least. Actually there are many suitable locations around your home. Perhaps the best spot for growing your orchids is under a tree which does not have too heavy a set of leaves and which allows sunlight to filter through all day. If you have only trees which give dense shade, then the plants should be hung or placed low-down beneath the tree where the morning and afternoon sun will come in under the leaves, but where the tree does give them shade during the middle of the day. If you do not have suitable trees, your orchids can be hung or set on the east side of your home where they will get most of the morning sun and where the house itself will shade them from the noonday and afternoon sun.

If you *remember that the plants want lots of sun but not more than one half of the full sun during the middle of the day from ten thirty until three,* I am sure that you will be able to find many suitable locations around your garden.

WATER   Water your orchids out of doors the same as you would when you are growing them indoors. *Water them heavily when you do water; don't water them again until they are bone dry.* The weather, however, will have a much greater effect on the growing conditions of orchids out of doors than it will on those in the home. In windy weather you may find it necessary to water much more often than normal. On the other hand, in rainy weather you may not have to water for several weeks at a time. If a rainy spell lasts for several weeks, it is usually better to take your plants indoors and allow them to dry out thoroughly every once in a while because the roots cannot stand staying wet for any length of time. In most sections of the United States there is no need to worry about humidity

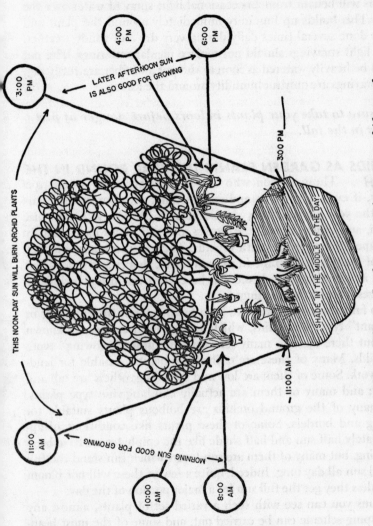

4. ORCHIDS UNDER TREES In the summertime your orchids can be taken outdoors and hung under a tree where they get at least half shade in the middle of the day.

THIS NOON-DAY SUN WILL BURN ORCHID PLANTS

LATER AFTERNOON SUN IS ALSO GOOD FOR GROWING

MORNING SUN GOOD FOR GROWING

SHADE IN THE MIDDLE OF THE DAY

for plants growing out of doors as there is usually a great plenty naturally present in the air. In very dry regions, however, plants out of doors will benefit from an occasional light spray of water over the leaves. This builds up humidity immediately around the plant and can be done several times daily during very dry and windy weather. These light sprayings should not replace regular waterings. The pot should be heavily watered as soon as the pot and fiber are really dry. The sprayings are only for humidity around the leaves.

Be sure to take your plants indoors before danger of first frost in the fall.

ORCHIDS AS GARDEN PLANTS THE YEAR ROUND IN THE SOUTH   Those of you who live in the far South where you seldom, if ever, have frosts and freezes can grow your orchids outdoors the year round. Many people here in Florida, in California, Hawaii, and other parts of the tropics and subtropics have actually landscaped their gardens with orchids. There are so many different types of orchids; they come in so many sizes, shapes and colors that almost any landscaping theme can be carried out using orchids as the largest part of the plantings.

So far in this book we have been talking about the epiphytic or "air plant" types of orchids, which are the most commonly known ones, but there are also many terrestrial or "ground-growing" types of orchids. Many of these are quite large plants, suitable for landscape work. Some of them are low and spreading; others are tall and slender; and many of them are actually climbing-vine type plants. Also many of the ground orchids are bulbous plants suitable for bedding and borders. Some of these plants like conditions of approximately half sun and half shade like the epiphytes we have been discussing, but many of them are sun lovers which can stand the full tropical sun all day long. Indeed, quite a few of these will not bloom well unless they get the full sun for a major portion of the day.

Thus you can see with such a varied set of plants, almost any landscaping scheme can be carried out, and some of the most beautiful gardens in Florida and Hawaii have been achieved almost solely with the use of orchids.

In regions where orchids can be grown outside all year round, many people prefer to grow the epiphytic types right on the trees in their gardens instead of in pots, using them as a permanent part of their landscaping. Of course, if you prefer, they can be kept in their pots and hung on the trees, and in some ways this is preferable because once the plants are rooted on the trees, they must stay there for good, whereas plants in pots can be used more flexibly —moved around from one spot to another, taken into the house when blooming, et cetera.

With such a varied group of plants, it is hard to give specific instructions for their care, but there are several general rules which can be noted.

ORCHIDS ON YOUR TREES   The care of the epiphyte types growing on the trees is essentially the same as when they are in pots with only minor changes.

WATER   When the plants are on the trees, their roots run out over the bark and are exposed to the air at all times. These exposed roots dry out much more quickly than roots in a pot. *This means that the plants will need considerably more water when growing on a tree than they do in the pot.* This is especially true when the plants are first put on the trees and until they develop a really well-established root system out over the bark of the tree. Once the plants become well established with a heavy root system, they can be left almost completely on their own (as the extensive root system picks up considerable moisture from dew and light rains), and they will need to be watered only during severe dry spells and extremely windy weather.

SUN   Conditions of sun and shade must be carefully considered before the plants are placed upon the tree to be sure that the location chosen is a suitable one. *Half sun and half shade during the middle of the day* at least is the important feature. Full sun early morning and late afternoon or all morning is usually all right, but the plants must have at least one-half shade during the middle of the day.

PLANTING ON THE TREES   The method used to fasten the plant to the tree is extremely important. *The plant must be so firmly attached that it cannot wiggle or move until it has rooted onto the tree.* The root tips of orchids are extremely tender and jelly-like in consistency, and the slightest movement as they begin to grow will

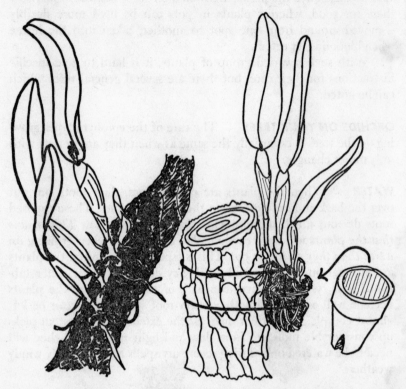

5. a) Orchid plant stapled onto tree limb, all osmunda removed from roots, plant on top side of limb growing upwards along the limb. b) Plant wired onto tree, osmunda ball left on roots, plant in upright position, new growths close to tree so that roots grow onto tree immediately.

break them and keep the plant from ever becoming firmly attached to the tree. The plant should be placed on the tree in such a way that it is as nearly upright as can be, and the growing front should be closest to the tree since the new roots will come from the new

Mrs. Burwin Bean and daughter showing one of their orchids — a *Cattleya trianaei* blooming for the third time in their home in Nebraska.

Mr. and Mrs. Ted Leitzell of Evanston, Illinois, in the orchid room of their home.

Photo by Chicago Tribune

Carefully packed orchid plants can be shipped anywhere with guaranteed safe delivery. They can even be shipped in bud to bloom soon after arrival. Plants come in the pot — all you have to do is unpack them, set them up in a sunny window and follow the simple growing instructions. Before you know it you have your own orchids.

The Starter Collection, arranged by the Fennell Orchid
Company of Homestead, Florida, as an introductory
offer to orchid-hobby beginners, consists of five *Cattleya*
plants — three of the regular lavenders (all mature to
bloom at different times around the year), and two almost full-grown seedlings (one a pure white, the other
dark to bloom within twelve to eighteen months); can be
bought for about $25.00. All five can be grown in one
window with little care and make a wonderful basis for
starting your collection.

growth and thus will attach to the tree as quickly as possible. If the plant is carefully and correctly attached to the tree, it will become established almost immediately and with little or no setback. Naturally, this is of greatest importance. Once the plant is well rooted onto the tree, the wires, staples, or other means used to fasten it tightly may be removed.

GROUND ORCHIDS The many types of terrestrial or semi-terrestrial orchids which can be grown in the soil like other garden plants can be divided roughly into four groups for cultural purposes. First of all, some types like half shade during the middle of the day at least, while others need full sun all day long. These two groups can again be divided into those which should be grown as actual ground plants in soil, and those which like a lighter and more open-growing medium than soil. These last are the so-called "semi-terrestrial" types, and the main difference between the two types is

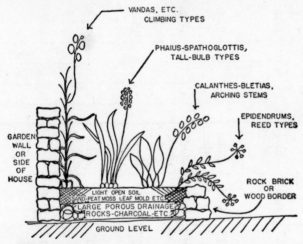

6. GROUND BED FOR TERRESTRIAL ORCHIDS.

that those which grow in soil like to be kept constantly damp at the roots, whereas the semi-terrestrial types, like the epiphytes, must dry out between waterings. The types which like constant moisture can be planted anywhere around the garden in regular soil. The other

GROUND ORCHIDS FOR THE GARDEN

Botanical Name (*Common Name*)	Color	Size	Number	Season	Monopodial	Sympodial	Evergreen	Deciduous	Size	Full	½	Keep Damp	Dry Out	Raised Bed	Ground	Border	Climber	Single	Comments
Arachnis several species and hybrids (Spider Orchid Scorpion Orchid)	yellow, green, brown, red, white lav.	2–4″	8–30	spring summer	x		x		2–10′	x			x	x			x	x	Striking, exotic flowers; last 1–2 months.
Bletia several species	white lav.	1–2″	6–10	winter spring		x		x	10–16″	x	x		x	x	x	x			Divide bulbs every year; double stock every year; very attractive.
Calanthe several species and hybrids	white red lav.	1½ to 3″	5–30	winter spring		x		x	12–24″	x	x		x	x	x	x			Flower when leaves drop; very attractive; divide bulbs every year; feed heavily.
Cymbidium many species and hybrids	all	1–5″	2–30	winter spring		x	x		12–30″	x	x		x	x	x	x		x	Very fine and beautiful; in cool but not cold climate; So. Cal. and sub-tropical mountain regions.
Cyrtopodium several species (Cowhorn or Beeswarm Orchid)	yellow brown	1–2″	many	spring		x		x	15–36″	x	x		x	x				x	Semi-terrestrial; must be well drained.
Dendrobiums many species and hybrids	all	1–4″	10–40			x	x		1–6′	x	x		x	x				x	Not really terrestrial; must be well drained; some of the cane types can be grown as semi-terrestrial; very beautiful and effective.
Epidendrum cane or reed stem types many species	all	¼ to 2″	many			x	x		1–4′	x		x		x	x	x			Very beautiful and effective; some types bloom constantly; one of the best for garden.

Genus	Color	Flower Size	No. of Flowers	Season	Plant Height	Remarks
Grammatophyllum several species	green brown	2–5″	many		3–8′	Very striking, effective, hard to bloom; tender to cold below 45° F.
Oncidiums several species and hybrids. (Dancing Doll, Dancing Lady, Spanish Dancing Girl)	yellow brown	1″	many		1–3′	Not really terrestrial. A few types—Altissimum-Sphacelatum group—can be grown in raised beds; must be well drained.
Phaius several species (Nuns Lily)	brown white	2–6″	6–20	spring summer	20–40″	Very stunning; easy to grow; can stand below freezing short while.
Renanthera several species and hybrids	red orange	1–3″	many	spring summer	6″–6′	Very fine and striking; easy to grow.
Sobralia several species	lav. white yellow	2–6″	2–3	summer fall	18″–4′	Very attractive; flowers last 1–3 days; bloom in succession for 2–3 weeks; hard to bloom.
Spathoglottis several species and hybrids	all	1–3″	many		1–3′	Very effective; one of best; easy to grow; stay in bloom months.
Thunia	white lav.	3–5″	2–10	summer	2–4′	Very attractive; hard to bloom; dry when leaves drop.
Vandas many species and hybrids	all	1–5″	6–30	any time	6″–15′	Finest; most beautiful of garden orchids; easy to grow; many bloom all the time, off and on, year round.
terete						Good for fences, wall, etc.
semi-terete						Good for fences, wall, etc.
strap leaves						Must be well drained. Like almost full sun.
Vanilla	green yellow	2–4″	5–15	spring summer	5′ and up	Interesting; pretty foliage, when climbing. Can produce own vanilla. Conversation piece.

types are usually grown in raised beds built up above ground level and filled with a light and open compost which drains quickly and therefore allows the roots to dry out between waterings. These beds are built above ground level rather than dug into the soil to insure quick and easy drainage. In all other respects these plants can be treated just like any of the rest of your garden plants.

In the chart on pages 20 and 21 I list a few of the more commonly available and easily grown types of orchids which are suitable for growing in the ground in gardens throughout the tropics and sub-tropics. For the most part this chart should be self-explanatory, but I will add a few supplementary notes.

WATER   In general, plants growing in the full sun will need more water than those growing under half-sun conditions.

SOIL   The soil used should be light and open or sandy so that the plants have good drainage at their roots. No orchids that I know of like soggy, wet conditions in which to grow.

COMPOST   The compost used in the raised beds can be made up of almost any materials which will not pack down to form a tight soil-like medium. Large rocks, chunks of charcoal, broken pots, gravel, and any other such substances can be mixed in liberally to insure the open conditions needed. Lawn clippings and prunings from the garden, peat moss, old osmunda fiber, leaf mold, coconut husks and other such compost should be added from time to time as needed.

The deciduous types (plants that drop all of their leaves during certain seasons every year) do not need water except when they are in active growth. When they drop their leaves, they are dormant like any other deciduous type of plant.

These terrestrial types of orchids can stand and do like considerable amounts of organic fertilizer. Frequent light applications of well-rotted manures or other organics can be applied, but care must be taken not to apply them heavily enough to start heating. Manure and many other organic fertilizers are high in nitrogen and low in potassium and phosphate so that it is definitely advisable to feed these terrestrial orchids with an inorganic fertilizer high in potassium and phosphate in addition to the organic fertilizers to insure strong growth and heavy blooming. Actually, a well-balanced inorganic plant food is all that is needed if applied regularly.

The second part of Chapter 9 discusses housing for the outdoor growing of orchids in the South when they are to be grown in pots rather than as an integral part of the garden landscaping.

chapter 3

Different Types of Orchids

THE ORCHID FAMILY   The orchid family is the largest of all plant families with fifteen thousand to eighteen thousand wild species (some botanists list as many as twenty thousand).

Orchids are found growing wild the world over from Arctic to Antarctic. There are many types of Northern orchids, such as the lady's-slippers. All of these are terrestrial, and a few of them have showy and interesting flowers. All of the orchids commonly known as corsage-type flowers and all of those suitable for growing in the home come from the tropics and sub-tropics, but most of these types are not truly tropical plants because in the wild they are found growing in mountainous regions from altitudes of three thousand to seven thousand feet and at such altitudes, even in the tropics, the plants do get occasional cold spells and once in a while even light freezes.

The large corsage-type orchids commonly seen at the florists' all come originally from South America, mostly from Columbia and Venezuela. Other types of orchids that we will discuss come from the Philippines, India, the Malay Peninsula, the South Sea Islands, Australia, Africa, Central America, and the West Indies.

Orchid plants range in height from less than an inch tall to eighteen feet or so, and the flowers themselves range from microscopic to almost a foot across. The flowers come in every conceivable hue of the rainbow. Some of them are one color all over; many of them are very strikingly spotted, striped, and otherwise figured. Many orchid flowers resemble other forms of nature and have both common names and botanical names derived from these forms. There are butterfly orchids, spider orchids, scorpion orchids, elephant orchids, tiger orchids, fox-tail orchids, dancing girl orchids, dove orchids, and countless others. Truly the orchid family is not only the largest, but also the most varied and widely distributed geographically of all plant families.

ORCHID NAMES

Orchid names are apt to be a bit confusing to the novice but actually there is nothing very different or difficult about them. Like people, orchids have several names. The first word of an orchid name is the Genus name and is like your family name. The second name is the species name—like your first name, thus, the names are simply reversed just as yours is when put in Alphabetical order in the phone book. People often have "nick names"; so do orchids. These we call common names to distinguish them from the scientific or botanical name. As with people, the common names don't mean much and the correct botanical name is the one you should try to learn. Common names can vary from one place to another and many of them are very general, applying equally well to many different orchids. Botanical names remain the same the world over, in all languages, and as such they mean something.

An example:

	Family Name	First Name	Nickname
People:	Smith	Tom	"Slim"

	Genus Name	Species Name	Common Name
Orchids:	*Cattleya*	*trianae*	"Christmas Orchid"

The genus name is usually in Greek—or based on the Greek language—and is usually a descriptive name describing some character of the plant or flower. The first letter is always capitalized. Sometimes the genus name is derived from the proper name of a person or place and given a Greek ending to make it conform to the rules of nomenclature. The species name is usually Latin, a descriptive term or a Latinized proper name. If it is a descriptive name it is not capitalized—if it is a Latinized proper name it is capitalized.

As you may guess from this method of naming it is very interesting to know what the names mean and how they were originally derived.

Orchid hybrids are named by the man who first blooms a new cross and, within certain bounds, he can name them as he sees fit. Many are named after their originators, et cetera. The genus name remains the same. The species name becomes a hybrid name and is usually capitalized.

METHOD OF GROWING   Most of the commonly grown types of orchids are epiphytes or "air plants" as they are commonly called. Actually the term "air plant" is misleading because orchid plants do not get any more food from the air than any other plant. Perhaps "perching plant" would be a better name for them as it more truly describes their method of growth. These epiphytes live and grow in elevated positions either on other trees and shrubs, or on the exposed surfaces of rock cliffs and outcroppings. The plants are not parasites; they do not take any food from the plant on which they grow but are merely using it to sit upon.

Orchid plants need the same mineral foods that other plants need. They merely get them in a slightly different way. Instead of sending their roots down into the soil to pick up the minerals orchid plants have a network of roots which they send out over the bark of the tree or rock on which they grow, and when it rains, dust which has blown up onto the tree is washed down to these roots. Also rotting bark and old leaves which get caught in the crotches of the tree above the plants and around and among the roots of the plant supply quite a bit of the food. When you stop to analyze the situation, it is evident that they can get a great deal of food by this method, and the mystery of how they grow up in the air is a mystery no more.

THE ANATOMY OF ORCHID PLANTS   Orchid plants are commonly divided into two groups as to their method of growth: those that grow in the ground—*terrestrials*; and those that grow in elevated positions on trees and rock cliffs, et cetera—*epiphytes*. Each of these groups is further divided into two types according to the structure of the plants.

Orchid plants having a central stem which grows straight up and lengthens indefinitely season after season are called *mono-*

podials. These monopodial orchids have leaves that are carried alternately on the central stem, and bloom stems come out of the central stem between the leaf and the stem. Most of these types also put out aerial roots where leaf and stem meet.

Orchid plants that have a creeping stem, from which many bulbs or stems grow upright, and which put out new growth periodically, usually on a seasonal basis, are called *sympodials.* The creeping stem or rhizome (as it is correctly named) can branch and grow in several directions. This type of plant grows new bulbs or stems, blooms on them, then grows a new set and blooms on these. The rhizome advances periodically in a lateral fashion as each new growth is made.

Thus with the two main groups, epiphytes and terrestrials, and their two sub-types, monopodials and sympodials, we have four basic types of orchid plant growth. These are: sympodial epiphytes, monopodial epiphytes, sympodial terrestrials, and monopodial terrestrials. Examples of all four of these types are quite common in orchid collections, but most of the commonly grown orchids are sympodial epiphytes.

SYMPODIAL GROWTH   The first set of drawings are of a sympodial, epiphytic orchid (*Cattleya*). The rhizome is the stem that creeps along the surface of the osmunda (black fern root fiber) in the pot. Note that this rhizome can branch as shown in Figure 8, b. The bulbs, or pseudo-bulbs as they are correctly called, grow up from this rhizome. The leaf (or leaves depending on the type of orchid) grows out at the top of the bulb. These leaves usually will last for several years, but some types of orchids are deciduous and drop their leaves every year. At the joint of bulb and leaf the flower sheath develops. This flower sheath is a leaflike envelope that protects the flower buds while they are forming. The buds grow up through this sheath and break out through the top. If a plant makes a flower sheath, it is a good sign that it is going to bloom. The buds take about six weeks to develop from the time that they are first visible at the bottom of the sheath until the flowers open. These buds do not necessarily start to develop as soon as the sheath forms, however, as some types wait for several months until their flowering season comes along.

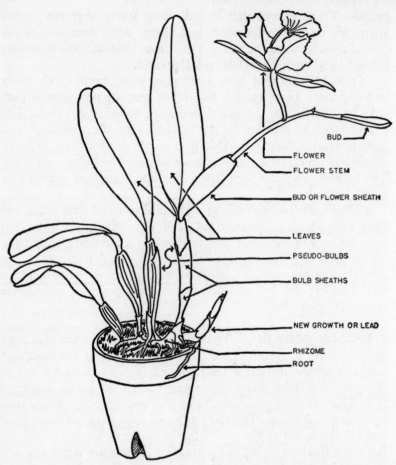

BUD

FLOWER

FLOWER STEM

BUD OR FLOWER SHEATH

LEAVES

PSEUDO-BULBS

BULB SHEATHS

NEW GROWTH OR LEAD

RHIZOME

ROOT

7. SYMPODIAL GROWTH, CATTLEYA ORCHID PLANT.

Life Cycle   At the bottom of the front, or lead, bulb there are two "eyes" or buds. These growing points will provide new growth which will bloom the next time. Normally only one of these buds develops into a new bulb (Fig. 8, a), and the other one stays dormant. These dormant buds will live for several years and can develop at any time if the plant is strong enough. Sometimes when a plant is growing strongly, both of the buds on the lead bulb will develop (Fig. 8, b). This results in a branching of the plant, and really strong plants will branch on almost every lead bulb (Fig. 8, d). As these new buds develop and grow, the rhizome slowly creeps across the pot. The old, or "back bulbs," at the back of the plant gradually weaken and die of old age. Usually the leaf turns yellow or brownish, shrivels and drops off. The bulb will usually live two or three years longer until it, too, shrivels and dies. This is a normal process and nothing to worry about as long as the plant is growing well at the front. A strong and healthy plant will usually put out two new growths for every one that dies, in this way steadily increasing in size. As long as the plant holds its own, it is doing all right, but if old bulbs die faster than new ones develop, something is wrong, and the plant and its growing conditions should be checked thoroughly for the reason.

MONOPODIAL GROWTH   (Figure 9, a) shows a monopodial (*Vanda*) type of orchid which could be either epiphytic or terrestrial. The growing point on monopodial plants is at the top of the central stem. This type of plant shows no definite seasonal growth. It grows constantly, steadily increasing in height when happy. Normal growth for monopodial orchids is straight up on a single stem (Fig. 9, a), but these plants can send out side shoots almost anywhere along the central stem. This does not happen too often as it takes some special incentive to start these side growths. Most monopodial types of orchids do not put out these side shoots easily or often. Perhaps the most common condition which induces the growth of side shoots is the injury or killing of the growing tip (Fig. 9, b). When this happens while the plant itself is still essentially strong and healthy, side shoots usually appear almost immediately and usually near the top of the central stem, just below the injured or dead tip. However, when monopodial plants get quite large and unusually strong, they will occasionally put out side shoots down at the bottom of the central stem (Fig. 9, c). Sometimes old and strong plants develop into really large and gorgeous specimens by this method. One *Vanda* at the Orchid Jungle which we have been growing for forty-five or fifty years has branched many times, and it is not at all unusual to see it in bloom with from 150 to 200 flowers at a time.

Eventually, as the plants continue upward, the leaves begin to die off at the bottom simply from old age, leaving a bare stem and the bottom roots which will continue to live for several years before they too slowly die of old age. This is natural and nothing to worry about as long as the plant is growing faster at the top than it is dying off at the bottom.

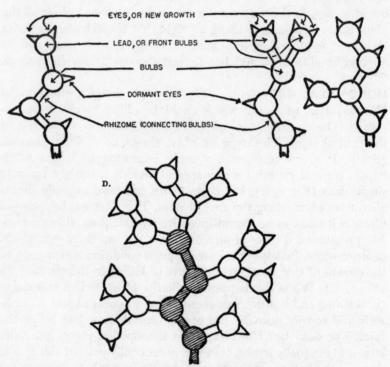

DIAGRAMATIC LIFE CYCLE

A. SINGLE PLANT   B. BRANCHED PLANT (FRONT)   C. BRANCHED PLANT
                                                              (SIDE BREAK)

EYES, OR NEW GROWTH

LEAD, OR FRONT BULBS

BULBS

DORMANT EYES

RHIZOME (CONNECTING BULBS)

D.

8.   METHODS OF SYMPODIAL BRANCHING.

Strong and healthy plants should increase in size steadily through this process. Most monopodial orchid plants are natural climbers; as the plant grows upward, aerial roots are produced constantly about a third to half of the way up the stem. These roots come out from the central stem between the leaves and steadily replace those which are dying off at the bottom.

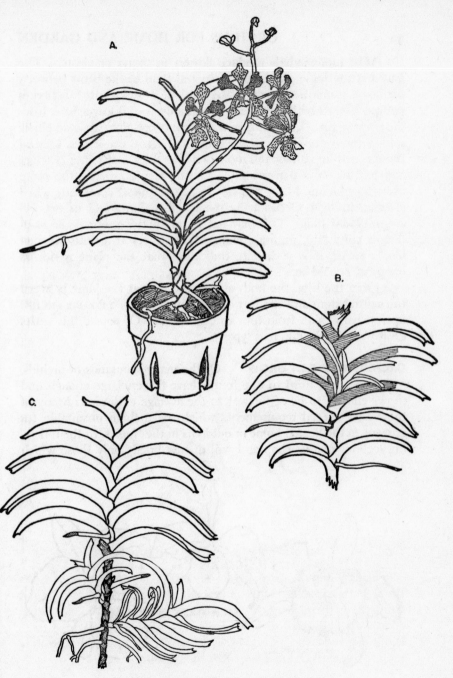

9. METHODS OF MONOPODIAL BRANCHING.

Most monopodials produce flowers in sprays or clusters. The flower stems come out from the central stem of the plant between the leaves somewhere towards the top half of the plant. Most types put out blooms with every leaf, but usually several leaves back from the growing tip. The blooms generally come out alternately on either side of the central stem in the same manner as the leaves. One of the nicest things about the monopodial orchids is that the stronger and healthier the plants are, the faster they grow and the more often they bloom. Many will stay in bloom almost constantly when growing strongly. Occasionally these plants skip a leaf or two between bloom stems. This may not mean anything, but if the skipping is consistent, jumping two or three leaves at a time between bloom stems, it is a definite indication that the plant is not as happy as it could be.

From the time the buds are first evident at the joint between the central stem and the leaf of the plant until the flowers are full open usually takes from four to eight weeks. Of course this varies greatly among the different types.

ORCHIDS YOU CAN GROW   Of the many thousands of orchids, only about one third to one fourth have flowers large enough and showy enough to be of interest to the average enthusiast. Many of these have special requirements which make them unsuitable for growing in the heated home or outdoors in the tropics. In the following sections of this chapter I will discuss briefly only those which

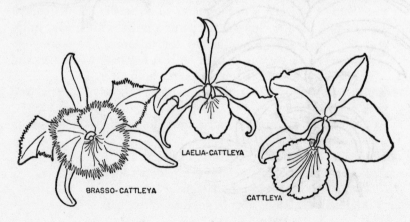

BRASSO-CATTLEYA

LAELIA-CATTLEYA

CATTLEYA

can be recommended for the beginner as house and garden plants.

There are four major groups of orchids which make up about 90 per cent of those grown commercially throughout the world. These four groups are in most ways the easiest to grow and the easiest for the beginner to obtain. By far the most popular and usually considered easiest to grow of all orchids is the *Cattleya* group.

GENUS *CATTLEYA*
Flowers

Color: predominantly lavender; many shades from blush pink to dark purple. Some albinos or pure whites and a few white with purple lip. Occasionally green and varying shades of yellow, tan, brown, bronze, and red. Some few are spotted or veined in contrasting colors.

Size: range from 1½ to 10 inches. Mostly in the 3- to 6-inch range.

Number of flowers: Commonly two to five per stem. A few of the cluster types have from five to thirty per stem.

Season: usually once a year. Each species has a distinct season, flowering within two to three weeks of the same time every year.

Plant

Type of growth: All *Cattleyas* are evergreen, sympodial epiphytes.

Size: normally 12 to 20 inches. A few dwarfs 4 to 8 inches. Some few reach a height of 24 to 48 inches. Plants consist of tall, usually club-shaped pseudo bulbs with heavy, leathery leaves, joined together by the rhizome. The more common types have one leaf per bulb. A few have two leaves and occasionally three to four leaves per bulb.

Natural habitat: foothills and mountainous regions of Central and South America.

Climate: two distinct rainy seasons alternating with severe dry seasons.

Culture: General culture described in Chapter 1 is ideal.

Potting: General instructions in Chapter 7 apply.

Container: usually pots or baskets

Material: Osmunda fiber or granulated tree bark.

GENUS CATTLEYA

BOTANICAL NAME (Common Name)	FLOWERS				PLANT			COMMENTS
	COLOR	SIZE	NUMBER	SEASON	SIZE	Single Leaf	Bi-foliate	
C. amethystoglossa	rose-lavender	4"	5–20	spring	18–30"		x	Very heavy substance; spotted; cut lip.
C. bicolor	bronze-green crimson lip	3–4"	5–15	summer	24–48"		x	Heavy substance; striking color; cut lip.
C. Bowringiana	lavender-purple	2–3"	10–25	autumn	12–30"		x	Strong and heavy grower.
C. dowiana	bright yellow, red veins, crimson and gold lip	4–7"	2–5	summer autumn	12–15"	x		Meager grower, most striking of all large *Cattleyas*.
C. Gaskelliana	medium to dark lavender	4–6"	3–6	late spring, early summer	10–14"	x		Small but compact grower; branches almost every lead. Floriferous.
var. alba	pure white							
C. gigas								Common name for *C. warscewiczii*.
C. guttata	yellowish tan with rust spots	3–4"	5–15	summer	18–36"		x	Cut lip—very heavy substance—waxy.
var. leopoldii	mahogany, heavily spotted with wine red, rosy purple lip							One of the most striking of all *Cattleyas* and rare; cut lip.
C. intermedia	blush white	3–4"	4–10	summer	10–15"		x	Heavy substance; cut lip. Used a great deal in hybrids for substance.
var. alba	pure white							
C. labiata	medium to dark lavender	5–7"	2–5	autumn	12–18"	x		All of the large flowered single-leaved species of *Cattleyas* are strictly speaking only botanical varieties of *C. labiata*. Thus these are often referred to as the labiata group.
var. alba	pure white							
C. Lueddemanniana	light to dark lavender	6–9"	2–7	winter, occasionally again in summer	10–16"	x		One of the finest of the labiata group but considered hard to grow. Actually grows well if given lots of sun and food and kept on the dry side.
var. alba	pure white							
C. Mendellii	blush white to light lavender dark lip	5–8"	2–4	late spring, summer	14–20"	x		Strong grower.
var. alba	pure white							

Name	Color	Flower size	No. flowers	Season	Plant height		Comments
C. *Mossiae* (Easter orchid)	medium to dark lavender	5–8″	3–7	Mar., Apr., May	12–18″	x	Strong grower and heavy bloomer.
var. *Wagenerii*	pure white						
C. *Percivaliana*	dark bright lavender, bright gold and crimson lip	4–6″	2–5	late fall and early winter		x	Very pretty striking colors, but unpleasant fragrance.
C. *Schroederae*	light blush lavender	4–7″	2–4	spring	14–20″	x	Vigorous grower, very pleasant aroma.
C. *Skinneri*	lavender	2–3″	4–20	spring	10–20″		Grows like a weed; very decorative.
var. *alba*	looks white	3–4″		autumn			Doesn't breed white.
var. *autumnalis*							Flowers larger; plants stronger; better substance.
C. *speciosissima*							Outdated synonym of C. *Luedemanniana*.
C. *trianaei* (Christmas orchid)	light blush to dark lavender	5–7″	2–5	Nov.–Feb.	14–24″	x	One of the most popular; best known; good one to start with. Will stand more abuse, less sun, and still bloom more than most orchids.
C. *Warscewiczii* (C. *gigas*)	medium to dark lavender	6–9″	2–10	summer	14–26	x	Very strong, heavy grower, bloomer. Needs lots of sun and food. Will stand full sun if accustomed to it gradually. Considered hard to grow; sun and food change this.

Relatives

Name	Color	Flower size	No. flowers	Season	Plant height		Comments
Brassavola B. *Digbyana*	greenish-white	4–7″	1–3	any time	8–15″	x	Lip large; deep-cut feathery edge—very striking; short, stocky, compact growing plants; leaves look dusty grey-green; bulb almost cylindrical; leaf heavy, short. Lots of sun, not much water; must dry out severely between waterings.
B. *glauca*	greenish-white	3–4″	1–2	spring	4–7″	x	Lip heart-shaped; heavy texture; dwarf stocky plants; dusty-looking grey-green leaves.
B. *nodosa* (Lady of the Night)	white lip, green sepals and petals	2–4″	2–5	autumn	6–9″	x	Lip heart-shaped; sepals and petals very thin; heavily scented at night; leaves long, blunt, almost cylindrical; bulbless; leaves on slender round stem.
Laelia L. *anceps*	lavender	3–4″	2–6 (spray)	autumn and winter	6–12″	x	Deeply corrugated bulbs; pointed leaves; long erect or arching spray of flowers; climber; better mounted than in pot; lots of sun—even full.
var. *alba*	white, red veins in lip						
var. *sanderiana*	white; purple lip						
L. *purpurata*	light blush to light lavender; dark lip	4–7″	3–9	spring	18–30″	x	Tall, slender plants; very striking flower, easy to grow.
var. *alba*	white; purple lip						Beautiful.
L. *tenebrosa*	yellow, tan, bronze, mahogany, purple lip	5–8″	2–6	winter spring	15–28″	x	Very unusual and striking color.

Relatives: The *Cattleyas* have several relatives. Only three are important: *Brassavola, Laelia* and *Sophronitis.*

The *Sophronitis* are difficult to grow and are seldom seen in cultivation, and their importance is solely for breeding purposes.

Most of the *Brassavolas* and *Laelias* resemble the *Cattleyas* closely, and they differ only in unimportant botanical ways.

Hybrids

The *Cattleya* group has been greatly increased through hybridization. There are many thousands of named *Cattleya* hybrids. Through hybridization we now have *Cattleyas* almost every size, shape and color. There are many hybrids in the *Cattleya* group resulting from crosses between the *Cattleyas* and their relatives. These are called bi-generic, tri-generic and poly-generic hybrids, et cetera. The most common of these are:

	Common Abbreviation
Brasso-cattleya	Bc.
Laelia-cattleya	Lc.
Brasso-laelia-cattleya	Blc.
Sophro-cattleya	Sc.
Sophro-laelia-cattleya	Slc.
Potinara (*Brasso-sophro-laelia-cattleya*)	Pot.

DENDROBIUM PAULINE

DENDROBIUM FIMBRIATUM, VARIETY OCULATUM

DENDROBIUM NOBILE

DENDROBIUM ROI ALBERT

The *Brassavolas* are used to give a large and more frilly throat. The *Sophronitis* have been used for bright, unusual colors in the yellow, orange, and red tones. The *Laelias* contribute heavy substance, unusual colors and free flowering, and the *Cattleyas* are used mainly for size and shape. Because of the great number and diversity of hybrids in the *Cattleya* group, none are listed in this book. It is enough to say that every grower will want to include some hybrids in his collection and should be able to make his own selection as his interest and collection grows.

GENUS DENDROBIUM
Flowers
Color: varying shades of lavender; also green, yellow, brown, rusty red, white.

Size: ½ inch to 4 inches.

Method of flowering: Usually long sprays with many flowers; occasionally short jointed stems, two to five flowers from each joint of the bulb; usually produced from top one half to two thirds of bulb.

Season: predominantly spring or autumn.

Plant
Type of growth: All *Dendrobiums* are sympodial plants; most are epiphytes; some are semi-terrestrial; about half are deciduous, half evergreen.

Size: Vary from dwarfs 2 to 8 inches tall to larger ones up to 9 feet tall. Most *Dendrobiums* have long slender cane stems or pseudo-bulbs; most are erect; some are pendant; many are jointed with a distinct zigzag effect. Most of these types have many leaves arranged opposite and alternate along the further two thirds of the bulb at least. Some few have short swollen bulblike pseudo bulbs with only one or two leaves.

Natural Habitat: Philippines, South Pacific islands, Australia, East Indies, Far East and India.

FOUR MAIN GROUPS
The *Dendrobiums* are easily divided into four main groups horticulturally:

1. **Nobile Group**   These are deciduous, semi-erect, or pendu-

GENUS DENDROBIUM

BOTANICAL NAME (Common Name)	COLOR	FLOWERS SIZE	NUMBER	SEASON	PLANT SIZE	COMMENTS
Nobile Group						
1. nobile	blush white; lavender tips and lip; maroon center	2–4"	2–5	winter spring	12–30"	Many stems of flowers per bulb; very showy; long zig-zag jointed bulbs; many leaves; deciduous second year; old bulbs will bloom for several years.
2. var. virginalis	pure white					Rare.
3. Pierardii	light lavender, sulphur yellow throat	1½–2"	2 per stem; many stems per bulb	winter spring	18"–6'	Plants completely pendant; very easy to grow; long slender bulbs ⅛" to ¼" in diameter; plants bloom when bare of leaves. Papery sheath; lower ⅔ of bulbs carry pair of flowers at each joint; very decorative.
4. superbum	lavender, dark maroon center	3–4"	2–5 per stem; many per bulb	winter spring	2'–6'	Bulbs ¼" to ⅝" in diameter; otherwise same as above; very fragrant.
5. var. dearei	absolutely pure white					Rare and very fine; also fragrant.
6. *Hybrids: There are many very fine hybrids, resulting in new shapes and colors, also larger and rounder flowers.*						
7. Adrasta	light lavender	2–2½"	2–5	spring	14–60"	Very showy hybrid of superbum and Pierardii; flowers and plant are intermediate between parents; strong grower; heavy bloomer; very attractive; blooms on bare bulbs.
8. Ainsworthiae	white-maroon center	3–4"	2–5 per stem; many stems	winter spring	12–30"	Culture like nobile; deciduous; needs dry period in fall.
9. Merlin	dark lavender	4–5"	2–5 per stem; many stems	winter spring		Culture like nobile; deciduous; needs dry period in fall.
10. Thwaitsiae	yellow; maroon center	2–3"	2–5 per stem	winter spring		Culture like nobile; deciduous; needs dry period in fall.
Evergreen Cane Group						
11. phalaenopsis	light to very dark lavender	2–4"	5–20	autumn	12–36"	Erect bulbs; many leaves; erect and arching flower sprays; flowers round and full—flat; last 6 weeks to 3 months. Culture like Cattleyas; can stand almost full sun.
12. var. alba	pure white					

	Color	Flower size		Season	Plant size	Description
13. Dixon's strain (var. of D. Phalaenopsis)	very dark lavender-purple	3–4"	5–20	autumn	12–30"	Darkest, most round and full of all Dendrobium Phalaenopsis types; very fine.
14. taurinum	rust red and yellow	1½–2"	15–30	any time	18–60"	Flowers twisted; very unusual and exotic; likes full sun all the time; grows well as semi-terrestrial in well-drained soil.
15. undulatum	tannish-green; lavender blush	1½–2"	15–30	any time	18–60"	Flowers twisted and undulating; very striking; strong grower; likes full sun and grows well as semi-terrestrial.
16. veratrifolium (antelope orchid)	green and white	2–3"	15–30	any time	24–60"	Flowers twisted; petals erect like antelope horns; lip shovel-shaped; very striking, decorative shape; can stand full sun; grows well as semi-terrestrial.
17. Hybrids: There are a great many in this group; only a few of the more common and easier ones to grow are listed here.						
18. Hawaii	lavender-purple	1½–3"	12–30	winter	12–48"	Large plants bloom almost all the time.
19. Lady Constance	very dark lavender purple	3½–4½"	10–20	any time autumn	12–40"	One of the largest, roundest, flatest of hybrids; very fine.
20. Lester McCoy	white and green or light lavender	1½–2½"	15–30	spring winter	14–48"	One of the most popular hybrids; flowers open and twisted; many are white; heavy bloomer; strong grower.
21. Liliha	very dark crimson purple	2½–4"	8–20	any time	14–48"	Fine hybrid; large, dark, flat, and nearly round flowers; blooms often.
22. Pauline	dark lavender all over	2–3"	15–20	autumn any time	18–60"	Blooms heavily; old bulbs bloom for several years.
23. Sander's Crimson	very dark crimson purple	3–4"	15–25	any time	18–60"	Buds drop off before opening in humid weather; large plants stay in bloom all the time.

Pendant Yellow Cluster Group

	Color	Flower size		Season	Plant size	Description
24. aggregatum	yellow and gold	1½–2"	6–20	spring	4–6"	Bulbs grow tightly packed together; dwarf plant; flower clusters—pendulous; lip large; almost hides sepals and petals; plant produces many stems of flowers; very cute and showy; a fine pot plant.
25. chrysotoxum	gold-yellow; orange lip	1½–2"	8–14	spring	12–24"	Very striking; fine; tall club-shaped bulbs; 3–6 leaves; flowers in arching sprays; last 10 days–2 weeks; bloom several times in spring; one-half to full sun, culture like Cattleyas, Chapter 1.
26. Dalhousianum	peach-maroon center	3–4½"	4–10	spring	18–72"	Large, semi-erect plant; very beautiful, heavy, waxy-looking flowers—bulbs covered silver sheaths with maroon stripes; leaves dark blue green, very handsome.
27. densiflorum	gold-yellow; orange lip	1½–2"	12–30	spring	12–24"	Very like Chrysotoxum except many more flowers; much closer together in cluster; culture same.
28. Farmeri	white or pink sepals and petals, gold lip	1½–2"	6–20	late spring	6–10"	Very cute; culture like Cattleyas; dwarf plant; flower cluster often as big as plant.
29. fimbriatum	yellow sepals and petals; gold lip	1½–2"	6–20	spring	18–40"	Strong grower; will take from one-half to full sun; many leaves; extremely decorative.

GENUS DENDROBIUM

BOTANICAL NAME (*Common Name*)	COLOR	FLOWERS SIZE	NUMBER	SEASON	PLANT SIZE	COMMENTS
30. var. *oculatum*	dark maroon eyes in lip	1½–2″				Flowers somewhat larger; more striking because of dark eyes.
31. *moschatum*	peach yellow	3–4″	5–14	spring	3–9′	Many leaves; long semi-pendant stems; pendant clusters; ½ to full sun. Deciduous second year.
32. *thyrsiflorum*	white sepals and petals orange lip	1½–2″	10–20	spring	14–30″	Plant grows and looks like *Densiflorum*; *Cattleya* culture.
Formosum Group						
33. *Dearei*	white	2–3″	2–5	summer	12–24	Looks very much like *formosum*, but bulbs are more slender and flowers smaller. Have black hairs on silver sheaths.
34. *formosum*	pure white	2–3″	2–5	autumn	10–26	Dark blue-green foliage; flowers last 2–3 months.
35. var. *gigantea*	pure white	3½–4½″	2–5	any time summer	10–26	Very nice; many leaves; dark blue-green; stem silver with black hairs; flowers last 2–3 months.
36. *Sanderae*	white	1½–2½″	2–5	any time	12–24″	Flowers larger; plants stronger than above; very fine. Very much like *Dearei*.

lous plants. They must be dried out severely in the fall from the time they finish growth until buds start. This drying out causes them to drop their leaves and forces them to bloom. If watered through the fall, these plants will continue to grow and put out little side-shoot plantlets instead of blooming. Many of the species in this group will thrive in full sun the year round, but actually, except for the severe drying, they may be grown just like *Cattleyas* (Chapter 1) and are well suited for home culture. The more common species are listed in the chart on page 36. There are many hybrids; a few are also listed. Nos. 1-10 in the chart are in this group.

2. *Evergreen Cane Group* These are erect cane type plants that are evergreen, keeping their leaves for several years. The plants themselves are quite attractive. Most are epiphytes, but many will do well as semi-terrestrial garden plants; unfortunately, with the exception of D. *Phalaenopsis*, most of these are large plants, too large for house plants. These types bloom with long, arching sprays of ten to thirty flowers, large plants often producing several sprays per bulb, and the same bulbs will often produce for several years. Several of the species will bloom two or three times a year, and many of the hybrids will stay in bloom almost constantly once they are full grown.

This evergreen branch of the *Dendrobium* family has just become popular in the last ten years, and now a great deal of hybridization is being done. Due to the size of the plants, only those with D. *Phalaenopsis* as ancestors are really suitable as house plants. The rest are primarily garden plants but will do well indoors or in a greenhouse if you have the room for them. All of this type do well under *Cattleya* culture (Chapter 1); most can stand full sun all day even in the tropics.

Nos. 11-23 in the chart are in this group.

3. *Pendant Yellow Cluster Group* These types are some of the most showy of all the *Dendrobiums*, but they have been neglected because their flowers have little or no commercial value. All are epiphytic sympodial plants. All of these types have pendant clusters of flowers; they range in size from 1½ to 4½ inches; the flowers are quite full, round and flat, and they vary in color considerably with yellow, peach and orange predominating. The lip of most of these types is cup- or pouch-shaped and very velvety. In most it is a deep orange color. The flowers last only about seven to ten days, however, and so have little commercial value. Most of these *Dendrobiums* bloom with several clusters in succession so that the plants actually stay in bloom for quite some time. All will do well under *Cattleya* culture (Chapter 1), but many can stand full sun all day long even in the tropics. Hybrids are few and far between in this group.

Actually, botanically speaking, this is not one group, but several. I have called them one group for convenience and simplicity. Nos. 24-32 in the chart are in this group.

4. Formosum Group   The plants in this group are all epiphytic sympodials; they have one easily distinguished feature—the bulb sheaths are covered and fringed with black hair. The flowers are predominantly white and look as if they were made of tissue paper; these flowers are quite large and last very well—two to three months. The formosum types are considered hard to grow but will do well if given *Cattleya* culture and a little extra feeding. They do well as house plants. Only four are commonly available—Nos. 33-36 in the chart.

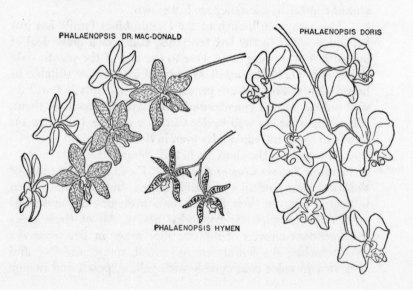

PHALAENOPSIS DR. MAC-DONALD

PHALAENOPSIS DORIS

PHALAENOPSIS HYMEN

GENUS *PHALAENOPSIS*

(called "Philippine Moth Orchid" or "Dogwood Orchid")
One of the best for home culture; one of the most beautiful
groups in the orchid family.

Flowers

Color: mostly white or lavender-pink; some have red markings,
spots and bars.

Size: vary from ¾ inch to 5 inches.

Method of flowering: long, arching sprays, sometimes branching; usually have many flowers; sometimes all at once; sometimes a few at a time for several months.

Plant

Type of growth: monopodial, epiphyte, evergreen.

Leaves: grow close together on short, central stem; usually
heavy, fleshy leaves, often one half as wide as long.

Roots: large and fleshy; green or gray.

Natural Habitat: mostly from Philippines; also East Indies and

Malay Peninsula.

Climate: most truly tropical of all commonly grown orchids.
Used to jungle conditions; high temperature and humidity,
lots of shade.

Culture

Sun: not more than one half full sun; can stand less than any
other orchid.

Water: have no storage capacities; want water regularly—lots
of it—but must be allowed to dry out between waterings.

Food: heavy; growth corresponds to amount of food available;
roots very tender to organic food.

Humidity: high—70% to 80%; 100% liable to result in leaf
rot; need good ventilation.

Potting

Container: pot, basket.

Material: Osmunda fiber is best. Charcoal and large, coarse
grades of bark with all of the fine particles removed, can be
used but osmunda still seems to work best with this group of
orchids. Repot every year in May or June as soon as new root
growth starts. Use large, firm chunks of osmunda cut to fit all
the way from top to bottom of pot with fibers running verti-

GENUS PHALAENOPSIS

BOTANICAL NAME (Common Name)	FLOWERS					PLANT	COMMENTS
	COLOR	SIZE	SHAPE	NUMBER	SEASON	LEAF LENGTH	
amabilis	white	3–4"	flat	10–30	winter	8–20" 2–5" wide	Largest and best of species.
esmeralda	pink to lavender, yellow lip	¾–1"	reflexed	many	autumn winter	4–7" 1" wide	Very cute; plants put out side-shoots easily; bloom on long branching stems a few flowers at a time for 3–5 months; large plants very decorative.
Lueddemanniana	yellow or cream, heavily spotted and barred, rust, red or wine	1½–2"	flat	3–12	spring summer	4–10" 2½–5" wide	Leaves wide; put out small plants on old bloom stems; so don't cut stems after blooming; flowers very heavy substance; bloom few at a time for 2 to 4 months.
rosea	light blush yellow lip	1–1½"	reflexed	many	year round	4–8" 1" wide	Only a few flowers at a time; stem grows and blooms year round; one plant author knows was in bloom five years, same stem.
Schilleriana	light to dark pink-lavender	2–4"	flat	15–100	winter spring	8–26" 2–6" wide	Very showy plant in or out of bloom; leaves light grey-green, heavily spotted and barred, dark green on top; bottom, wine purple all over. Large plants can bloom with two or three stems of 100 flowers each.
Stuartiana	white, spotted red	2–4"	flat	15–100	winter spring	8–26" 2–6" wide	Same as above.

Hybrids: Many fine hybrids; much more available than species; have much larger and finer flowers, not usually as many per stem.

Name	Color	Flower size	Per stem	Width	Description
Chieftain	white	4–5½"	8–20	8–26" / 3–6" wide / 8–25"	Clear, green leaves.
Confirmation	light pink to white	3–4"	15–50	3–6" wide	Spotted leaves, very nice.
Doris	white, occasionally some pink	4–5"	8–20	3–6" wide	Best known; one of the most popular; clear green leaves.
La Canada	white	4–5"	8–20	3–6" wide	Clear green leaves.
Pamela	light pink	3–4"	10–30	3–6" wide	Spotted leaves.
Psyche	white	3–4½"	10–30	3–6" wide	Clear green leaves.
Reve Rose	dark pink	3–4"	15–50	3–6" wide	Dark spotted leaves; best of all pinks; heavy texture and round flowers.
Rothomago	dark pink	2½–3½"	15–50	3–6" wide	Dark spotted leaves; good pink.
Winged Victory	white	4–5½"	10–20	3–6" wide	Supposed to be one of largest *Phalaenopsis.*

13. *PHALAENOPSIS DORIS*—showing bloom stems in various stages. *Left*—normal stem in bloom, *Center, bottom*—new bloom stem just starting, *Right*—an old bloom stem cut off behind lowest flower after blooming is finished—strong plants such as this throw a side break or "forced" bloom stem from one of the dormant eyes along the lower half of the old stem. By continued cutting back like this, large plants can be kept in bloom the year around. One stem will sometimes bloom for three to four years. Only large, strong plants on a heavy feeding schedule should be kept in bloom like this year after year.

cally. Hold plant in center of pot, fill in around with only 3 to 5 large, hard chunks of osmunda leaving an open space in center around the central stem of the plant and open spaces between the chunks. Pot the chunks just tightly enough together to hold the plant in place. You will find that the open spaces form vapor chambers which attract the new roots. These grow into the spaces, then root into osmunda chunks along the walls of the spaces.

With constant dampness and heavier watering used on *Phalaenopsis* the fiber deteriorates more quickly than usual. It may still look pretty good after one year but it will not last well through the second year, so it is definitely advisable to repot every year. Best time is in MAY-JUNE when new root growth starts.

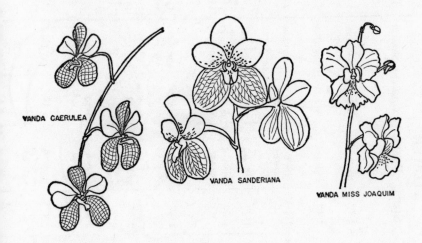

VANDA CAERULEA

VANDA SANDERIANA

VANDA MISS JOAQUIM

GENUS VANDA

The latest craze among orchid collectors; in many ways the *Vandas* are the most satisfactory of all orchids for home and hobby growing.

Flowers

Color: Actually every color of the rainbow; predominantly lavender-blue and yellow-brown in cultivation.

Size—shape: Vary from 1 to 6½ inches. Usually rather flat flow-

GENUS VANDA

BOTANICAL NAME (Common Name)	FLOWER					PLANT		COMMENTS
	COLOR	SIZE	SHAPE	NUMBER	SEASON	LEAF SIZE	HEIGHT	
coerulea	sky blue	3–4"	flat	8–20	autumn winter	1 x 6–10"	12–50"	Very beautiful and popular; the only true blue orchid; somewhat tricky to grow. Likes cool conditions.
Dearei	yellow	3–4"	reflexed	4–8	any time	3 x 15"	24–72"	Very heavy, closely leaved plant; blooms on every leaf year round; fragrance like lemon juice.
luzonica	cream with wine spots and bars at tips of sepals and petals.	2½–4"	reflexed and twisted	8–15	any time	2 x 14"	14–60"	Very stunning flower; rare and fine.
Merrillii	dark Chinese red on yellow	1½"	reflexed	8–15	summer autumn	1½ x 12"	12–48"	Striking flower; heavy texture; rare and nice.
Sanderiana	cream or pink background; terracotta veins on bottom sepals and petals.	4–6"	flat and round	6–15	summer winter	1½ x 14	7–30"	Considered finest of all vandas; one of most popular; slow and sometimes tricky to grow; likes lots of sun; good ones are dark pink and terracotta and so round and full that sepals and petals overlap.
spathulata	bright yellow	1½"	slightly reflexed	few at a time several months	summer any time	½ x 4–6"	18–72"	Rare; very attractive; likes shade on lower plant but must have full sun at top in order to bloom.
suavis	cream, rust-brown spots	2–3"	reflexed and twisted	6–12	any time	1½ x 18"	14–120"	Plants branch easily; make large and showy plants; bloom on every leaf; large ones bloom all the time; year round; heavy sweet odor.
teres	dark lav.	2–4"	large cone-shaped lip	2–10	spring summer	¼ x 3"	14–60"	Tall slender plants; cylindrical leaves; called terete leaves; not good out of Florida or sub-tropics; needs full tropical sun to bloom.
Tricolor	cream, rust-brown spots; lav. edge on sepals and petals; lavender lip	3–4"	reflexed and twisted	6–12	any time	1½ x 18"	14–120"	Strong grower; can stand one-half to full sun; blooms every leaf; large plants, all the time; very nice fragrance of grape-juice.

V. *Suavis*, which result in hybrids that bloom the year round, and ones resulting from crosses of *V. Sanderiana* which are large, flat, and round but bloom only one or two times a year. Probably the best and most popular of both of these types are crosses with *V. Coerulea* which produce blues and rosy pinks.

There are also a great many terete and semi-terete hybrids—good, often-blooming garden plants but will not bloom up north or indoors at all.

Relatives: The Vandas have a great many fascinating relatives; only a few of the more common and important ones are listed here.

Aerides odoratum	cream, lavender tips	1–1½"	10–30	summer	1¼ x 8–12"	6–24"	Culture like *Cattleyas*; flowers look like elephant head; trunk, ears, and all. Long drooping sprays; very fragrant; unusual and attractive.
Angraecum eburneum	light apple green, white lip	3–4"	15–25	winter spring	2½ x 20"	18–60"	Large, heavy, closely leaved plant; long arching sprays of heavy, waxy flowers; very exotic; rare, culture like *Cattleyas*.
sesquipedale	greenish white	5–8"	2–5	spring	2 x 10–16"	10–30"	One of the most unusual of all orchids; has a long tail on back of lip; up to 18" long; very tailored or modernistic looking flower; heavy and waxy; rare; very fine; culture like *Cattleya*.
Arachnis Hookeriana	pure white	2–4"	10–30	summer	1 x 6–8"	30–72"	Tall, leggy plants; 2–6" between leaves along stem; large widely branched spray of flowers. Needs full tropical sun all day long to bloom.
moschifera (Scorpion Orchid)	yellow-green; dark blood red bars	3–4½"	10–30	summer any time	1 x 8"	48–90"	Very exotic; heavy waxy flower; when worn is often mistaken for enameled costume jewelry.
Renanthera coccinea	orangy blood red	2½–3"	25–60	winter spring	¾ x 6–8"	24–72"	Tall, leggy plant; 1–2" between leaves; needs full sun; lots of water and food; very striking; fine.
Imschootiana	dark blood red	2–2½"	10–30	spring summer		8–36"	Dwarf growing; heavy bloomer; will do well in one-half sun; can stand full sun; very fine; gorgeous; rare.
Storeii	orange red	3–4"	25–75	winter spring	1½ x 10–12"	30–90"	Giant plant—4–6" between leaves; will grow and bloom in ½ sun; prefers full sun all day; lots of water and food.
Saccolabium giganteum	light lav.	1–1½"	25–60	winter	1½ x 10–12"	6–15"	Heavy, closely leaved plant; flowers tightly packed together on long spray; spicy fragrance; very cute; quite showy.

ers but often with twisted petals and sometimes quite re-
flexed.

Method of flowering: Flowers on long, erect, or arching sprays.
Usually quite a few flowers; some types only a few at a time,
but stems grow and continue to bloom for several months.

Season: Some *Vandas* have definite seasons; many will bloom
any time; large and strong plants bloom almost constantly.

Plant

Type of growth: monopodial evergreen—epiphytes, terrestrials
and semi-terrestrials. (Actually most *Vandas* are climbing
vines that start out on the ground as terrestrials or semi-
terrestrials and end up in the trees as complete epiphytes.
Few of them like actual soil, but almost all will grow in any
light, open compost, such as leaf mold.)

Size: Vary from a few inches in height to 7 to 10 feet tall.

Leaves: Produced opposite and alternate along the central stem.
There are three types:

terete leaves—short, cylindrical, pencil-like.

strap leaves—long, usually narrow and arching, make a beau-
tifully graceful plant; one of the few types of orchid that is
really attractive even when not in bloom. The ends of strap
leaves are notched, often seem to have been chewed off by
an insect or mouse.

semi-terete leaves—result of cross breeding between two types
above; usually short, V-shaped and deeply channeled in cross
section; usually pointed.

Roots: large, heavy, fleshy roots; many reaching straight out
into the air as aerial feeders. Do not like to be disturbed;
plant doesn't put out many; not replaced easily; roots branch
often.

Natural Habitat: Far East, East Indies, Malay Peninsula and Philippines.

Climate: fairly constant supply of rain and humidity without
severe dry spells or drastic changes of temperature; some, however, are from the mountains and can stand low temperatures.
Like lots of sun.

Culture: Can be grown with *Cattleyas*. Same culture.

Sun: Most *Vandas* will do well with one-half sun but will bloom

Cattleya lueddemanniana — Blooming on a tree at the Orchid Jungle. Notice how the roots cling to the tree and grow up and down the trunk collecting food and moisture.

Orchids in the Garden – a beautiful Orchid Show exhibit showing how these plants can be used in landscaping.

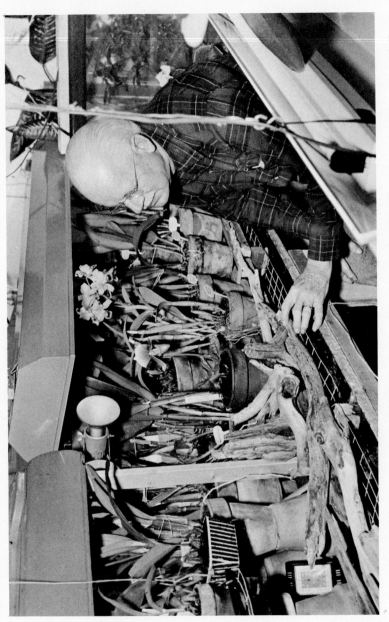

Mr. Roger Clark of Marblehead, Mass., in his basement orchid room where he has successfully grown orchids under artificial light for several years.

Orchids in a Sunny Window — showing the Cake Pan Method of growing orchids in your home. Notice that the table is directly in front of the window and right up against the wall so that the plants receive direct sun. Notice also that the pots are sitting on top of the gravel above the water level in the Pyrex cake pans. More decorative containers, such as the Chinese bowl in the center foreground can also be used as long as they are wide and shallow, allowing good ventilation around the pot, but care must be taken to be sure that the water level in the gravel does not come up to the bottom of the pot.

more with larger and darker flowers if they get almost full sun with only a little shade in the middle of the day; many actually do well in the full tropical sun all day long.

Water: *Vandas* like lots of water, but they cannot stand staying wet at the roots; they should be very well drained.

Food: *Vandas* will take all they can get of almost any type; inorganic preferred because it is not so likely to start fungus leaf and root infections.

Potting: *Vanda* roots don't like to be disturbed; put in large, well-drained and ventilated container and don't bother them.

Container: Pot or basket; a totem pole or upright stake of some porous material for the aerial roots to attach to will be appreciated.

Material: *Vandas* don't like osmunda once they begin to reach maturity; they want more open conditions. Usually potted in large lump charcoal with open spaces between lumps; charcoal doesn't rot; if large pot is used, won't need repotting for ten to fifteen years.

NOTE: Charcoal doesn't hold much water; plants can be watered almost every sunny day. Many growers in Hawaii and almost all growers here in Florida now use this charcoal potting method.

Hybrids   The field of breeding the *Vandas* and their relatives has just started. There are already many bi-generic hybrids and a few tri-generic hybrids. *Vanda* × *Aerides* = *Aeridovanda*; *Vanda* × *Arachnis* = *Aranda*; *Vanda* × *Renanthera* = *Renantanda*. Some weird and wonderful combinations of colors and shapes have been produced, and many more will be as the work progresses. As yet most of these hybrids are very rare and expensive, so we will not list many of them here. It is enough to say that the field is almost unlimited, and great things can be expected of this group of orchids in the years to come.

BOTANICAL ORCHIDS
Unusual Collector's Items   The orchids described so far have all been the larger and showier types that are grown for cut-flower purposes. These are the types that are grown by the commercial men, and most of them are fairly common and easy to find and buy. They

BOTANICAL ORCHIDS

Botanical Name (Common Name)	FLOWERS					Origin	PLANT						Size	Comments
	Color	Size	Shape	Number	Season		Epiphyte	Terrestrial	Monopodial	Sympodial	Deciduous	Evergreen		
Aerides *Angraecum* *Arachnis*							x x		x x x			x x x		See *Vanda* Group. See *Vanda* Group. See *Vanda* Group—see chart in Chapter 2.
Bletia patula	purple	2"	like *Cattleya*	6-10	winter spring	West Indies		x		x	x		14-20"	Flowers on erect stem; see chart in Chapter 2.
Brassavola *Brassia* several species	yellow, green, brown spots	3-8"	spider	10-20	spring summer	Latin America	x x			x x		x x	10-16"	See *Cattleya* group. Very striking and exotic flowers; spotted and barred in striking designs.
Calanthe several species and hybrids	white, red, and lavender	1½-3"		5-30	winter spring	East India, Philippines etc.		x		x	x		12-24"	Flowers long lasting; blooms after foliage drops; very attractive pot plant.
Catasetum several species	green, yellow and brown	1½-3"	pouch lip	3-12		Latin America	x			x	x		12-24"	Weird; flowers spit or throw pollen when a trigger is touched; very few are attractive, flowers seldom open fully.
Chysis bractescens	white	3-4"	round	2-8	spring summer	Mexico	x			x	x		14-24"	Plants grow upside down; bulbs long banana-shaped, hang down; leaves light, wide, paper-thin.
aurea	yellow, blush red	1-2"	round	2-8	spring summer	Mexico	x			x				Bulbs long, slender.
Coelogyne many species	mostly white or green	1-4"	like *Cattleya*	2-20		Far East	x			x	x			Many fascinating species; most cool growing; not suitable for home; some striped with black on green.
corrugata	white	1½"		4-8								x		Easy to grow in home; very cute; flowers on hanging stem.
Cycnoches several species (Swan Orchid)	green	1-5"	swan	5-60		Central America	x					x	6-36"	Very stunning; exotic flower shaped like a swan; heavy; lasts well; fragrant; sometimes difficult to grow. Flowers occasionally pink or brownish-purple.
Cymbidiums many species and hybrids	white, green, yellow, pink	1-5"	star	2-30	winter spring	Far East		x		x	x		12-30"	Listed as botanicals because cannot be advised in home; most need cool conditions; are grown commercially in Cal. and the north. Flowers last for months; very fine but not f⸻

Continuation of orchid chart. The original page is a rotated (landscape) table; several culture-category columns marked with "x" appear between "Origin" and "Plant size," but their column headers are cut off at the top of the page. The readable data follows:

Name	Color	Flower size	Lip	No. of flowers	Season	Origin	Plant size	Comments
many species and hybrids (Lady's Slippers)			slipper					...home culture; plants are delicate; many need cool conditions; flowers last well, are very striking and fascinating group.
Cyrtopodium — several species (Cigar Orchid)	yellow, brown or red	1–2"	like Cattleya	many	spring	Latin America	15–36"	Bulbs cigar-shaped; covered silver paper; leaves fan out from bulb top; large sprays of flowers; very striking; last 1–2 weeks.
Diacrium — several species (Virgin Orchid)	white	1–2"	like Phal.	10–30	spring	Latin America	10–20"	Bulbs hollow; flowers last well; very attractive.
Epidendrum — many species and hybrids	all colors	¼–3"		few to many		Latin America		One of largest groups in orchid family; vary greatly; many are beautiful; many are very exotic; many make beautiful house pot plants; some are good garden plants.
two common types: cane or reed stem	all colors	¼–2"		many in cluster few to many			6–30"	See chart, Chapter 2.
bulb types	all colors	¼–3"				Latin America	6–20"	Many exotic and wonderful flower types; most are good pot plants; some need cool conditions.
Gongora — several species (Punch & Judy orchid)	yellow, brown, red	1–2"	turn inside out shovel lip	many		Latin America		Unusual; not pretty; flower stems long, hang down. Called "Punch & Judy" orchid—flowers look like Marionette faces. See Chapter 2 chart.
Grammatophyllum	green spotted, barred brown	2–5"	like Cattleya	many		Philippines	3–8'	Very large growing—flower spikes 3–6' long. Very striking.
Laelia	green, yellow, white	1–4"	triangular	2–10	winter spring	Latin America	10–20"	Very striking; pretty flowers; fragrant; some need cool conditions.
Lycaste — several species	all	1–4"		1–12		Latin America		Many striking and beautiful types; almost all need cool conditions; not for home.
Miltonia — many species and hybrids	all; lots of red	1–6"	frilly full	3 to many	winter spring	Latin America	6–16"	Many very gorgeous; all cool types; not for home.
Odontoglossum — many species and hybrids						Latin America		
Oncidium — many species and hybrids (Dancing Lady, Shower of Gold, and Butterfly Orchids.)	mostly yellow and brown; some white and lavender.	¼–4"	usually have doll-shaped lip	1 to many		Latin America	2"–2'	One of largest; most fascinating of all groups; almost all are stunning exotic flowers; some few are cool growing types. Most will take full sun even in tropics; easy to grow; good pot plants; don't repot often.
Phaius — several species (Nun's Lily)	mostly brown and wht. lav. lip	2–6"	like Cattleya	6–20	spring summer	Far East and Philippines	20–40"	Easy to grow; erect flower stems; very attractive. See chart, Chapter 2.
Renanthera								See Vanda group.
Saccolabium								See Vanda group.

BOTANICAL ORCHIDS

Botanical Name (Common Name)	Flowers					Origin	Plant						Size	Comments
	Color	Size	Shape	Number	Season		Epiphyte	Terrestrial	Monopodial	Sympodial	Deciduous	Evergreen		
Schomburgkia several species (Cow's Horn Orchid)	all	1–4"	twisted and curled	6–30		Latin America	x			x		x	6–24"	Hollow bulbs; long erect flower stem; cluster of flowers at top; very fascinating, attractive flowers; most like full sun in tropics.
Sobralia several species	lavender, white, yellow	2–6"	like *Cattleya*	2–3	summer fall	Latin America		x		x		x	18–48"	Tall slender cane stems—like bamboo; flowers last 1–3 days. See chart, Chapter 2.
Sophronitis Spathoglottis many species	all	1–3"	many	1–7		Far East	x	x		x	x	x	12–30"	Very attractive garden or pot plants; bloom one year from seed; see chart, Chapter 2. See *Cattleya* group.
Stanhopea several species and hybrids (Dragon Orchid)	white, yellow, green, and brown spotted	3–8"	like dragon head	1–7	summer fall	Latin America	x			x		x	10–16"	Plant in baskets; flowers come out from below through roots and potting material; hang down; very striking, exotic, flowers last 3–7 days.
Thunia several species	white, lavender	3–5"	like *Cattleya*	2–10	summer	Far East		x		x	x		2–4'	Bulbs live only one year—till new bulb is made; hard to flower; very pretty flowers; last 7–10 days.
Vanilla several species	white, green, yellow	2–4"	like *Cattleya*	5–15	spring summer	Latin America		x	x			x	5' and up	Climbing vine; seed pod is vanilla bean; all genuine vanilla extract made from it; flowers last 1–2 days; wants shade, humidity, heat, water.

make up at least 90 per cent of the orchids in cultivation, but actually they are only a very small part of the orchid family. By far the largest part of the orchid family has flowers that are too small, too unusual, or that don't last long enough for florist use.

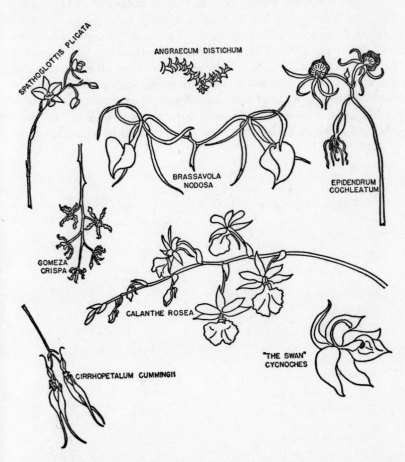

These seldom-grown types are usually lumped into one general group called "botanicals." Commercial men as a rule can't afford to waste space, time and effort growing these orchids which produce flowers they can't sell. This is a shame because most of the really charming and fascinating members of the orchid family are in this group. Luckily, many hobbyists the world over have developed a definite interest in these plants, and I am sure that as hobby growing increases, we will see more and more of these exotic and intriguing orchids.

Some botanists list as many as twenty thousand to twenty-five thousand botanical species of orchids. The list on pages 52-53 is only a brief introduction to this group, but I am sure the small taste given here will whet the hobbyist's appetite for knowing and acquiring more of these rare and wonderful plants. Almost all of those listed are interesting, worth-while, easy to grow, and available on the market. Just one word of warning—if you do get interested in these orchids, you'll have your life work cut out for you. You can't possibly get all of them, but you may spend the rest of your life trying.

chapter 4

How to Buy Orchids

PRICE   Orchid plants vary greatly in price from as little as 50 cents to as much as $2,500. Most desirable and commercially grown orchids, however, can be purchased at prices ranging from $8.50 to $25 apiece. There is a very good selection in this price range for the average grower, and even the avid collector seldom will find it necessary to go much above this price. Larger plants and individuals of very fine quality sometimes run as high as $75. Higher prices than this are sometimes paid by commercial orchid breeders and large collectors for plants which will be used for breeding and for show. Such plants are few and far between.

Many factors determine the value of orchid plants.

Rarity of course is important in determining price. Plants which are rare in the wild and plants that for one reason or another are seldom cultivated do bring higher prices.

Size and strength of a plant also determine price, and this is often ignored by the beginner. A large plant of several leads is naturally worth several times as much as a single lead plant, and small divisions are worth considerably less. When buying a plant, a great deal of attention should be given to its size, strength and health. Strong, healthy plants will continue to grow and bloom better than small, weak or sickly ones. This is especially important to the beginner as a start with sickly and weak plants is a poor start indeed. Don't start off with three strikes against you. Make sure that your first plants are strong ones, and your chances for success from the beginning will be much better. Buying small, weak plants to begin with because they are cheaper is penny wise and pound foolish.

Try to pick plants that have well-filled-out, plump, bulbs and firm leaves.

Plant color is also an important indication of strength and health. Strong, healthy plants are usually a bright green in color, whereas sick ones are more likely to be either light yellowish green, or a dark velvety green.

Roots—One other point on plant health that should be considered is the condition of the roots. Healthy orchid roots are firm, white or light green in color, and should be evident throughout the pot and fiber. If the plant does not have a strong, healthy set of roots, it cannot be expected to grow well.

Most people are inclined to buy plants without carefully considering those points of strength and health, but it is not wise to do so. More than anything else, the health and strength of your plants to begin with will determine your future results.

Ease of culture has a great deal to do with the price of orchid plants. Naturally those that are easiest to grow are more common commercially and therefore are inclined to be less expensive than those which are hard to grow.

The type of flower that an orchid plant produces also has a lot to do with the plant's value. The orchid family is usually divided into two groups according to flower types: those plants which produce flowers of commercial value suitable for corsages and florist work; and those which produce flowers of botanical or collector's interest only. The value of the botanical plants is usually determined mainly by the rarity, size and strength of the plant and its ease of culture. Plants which produce flowers of commercial value, however, are usually priced mainly from the standpoint of flower quality and only secondarily by the standards of rarity, size of plant and ease of culture. Several combined characteristics determine the quality of individual flowers.

Flower shape is very important. Flowers should hold themselves erect in a fully opened position. Ideal shape for most orchids is generally considered to be a flower which has its individual sepals, petals and lip held closely together in an almost flat or slightly dished position. The sepals, petals and

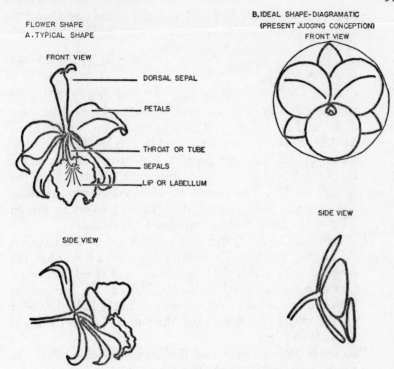

FLOWER SHAPE
A. TYPICAL SHAPE

FRONT VIEW

DORSAL SEPAL

PETALS

THROAT OR TUBE

SEPALS

LIP OR LABELLUM

SIDE VIEW

B. IDEAL SHAPE-DIAGRAMATIC
(PRESENT JUDGING CONCEPTION)
FRONT VIEW

SIDE VIEW

16.   FLOWER SHAPE, TYPICAL, IDEAL.

lip should be wide enough and held in such a position that they form a nearly complete circle in silhouette. (Sepals and petals should be relatively flat and straight. Curling of sepal tips and edges backwards is considered undersirable. Gentle undulations and small ruffling of the edges of the petals is desirable. Petals that curl backwards or that droop downwards at the tips and petals that do not open out as far as the sepals are undesirable.) The size and shape of the lip is also important to the over-all shape of the flower. The lip should be roughly of the same general size as one of the petals, and ruffling or lacy-cut edges are considered desirable. It is desirable that the tube of the lip should be closed over the column all of the way down. Figure 16 illustrates several of these points. In short, *the best-shaped flower is the one closest to a complete circle, slightly dished, and with well-balanced position and size of sepals, petals and lip.*

Size also determines the quality of a flower—in general, the bigger, the better.

Color is another important part of flower quality. Extremes and novelties in color are most desirable. Pure white, very dark, reddish, yellow and bronze tones are sought after. Medium-lavender or orchid-colored flowers are the most common, yet still the most popular. Contrasting colors in the lip of the flower are extremely important in determining the flower's quality. Two points are considered here—harmony and contrast. Bold and bright contrasting colors in the lip liven up the flower and are considered very desirable.

The substance of the flower is also important as it determines the keeping qualities. The heavier substance a flower has, the longer it will last and the more abuse it will stand. This question of substance is extremely important to the commercial man and also should be of importance to the hobbyist. After all, the longer your flowers last, the more enjoyment you will derive from them.

*Two other factors—stem and floriferousness—*also affect the value of an orchid plant. The flower stem is important because of the way it supports the blossoms. A strong, stiff stem will hold them upright in an attractive and well-spaced manner. The stems should be long enough to allow the flowers sufficient space in which to open fully. If the stems are short or weak and droopy, the flowers will be crowded together so that they are hard to see, hard to appreciate fully, and so that it is impossible for them to open completely. Floriferousness is also important both to hobbyists and professional men because we all want as many flowers as possible. There are two considerations here—how many flowers a plant produces per stem, and how many stems a year it produces.

This whole discussion on flower quality is based on what orchid growers consider to be the ideal flower. Few if any orchid plants produce perfect or ideal flowers. Almost all orchids fall short in one respect or another. A plant which produced flowers with all of the desirable qualities listed above would be worth hundreds of dollars. The price of the plants you buy is usually based on these standards. The more of these desirable qualities a flower has, the more expensive the plant will be. *Remember this when you price a plant.*

Some of the points discussed above may seem unimportant to the beginner at first glance, but actually they make sense when you stop to think about them. The more interested you become in your orchids, the more these points will mean to you.

BEWARE   There is one other factor which sometimes plays a large part in pricing orchids, and unfortunately, on the whole, it is a very artificial point of view. Every once in a while some particular orchid will gain an unduly high reputation or "name." A few exceptionally fine plants out of a group of average quality will receive several awards at orchid shows, and because of the resulting publicity this reputation or name becomes impressed on the beginner's mind. Consequently many growers will want one of these plants, and the price of the strictly average individuals of the same name will skyrocket. In the past few years this artificial situation has developed several times, and many average plants have sold at quite high prices, while others of equal—and oftentimes even finer—quality but of different names have been available much less expensively. *When buying a particular plant by name it is well to find out about the flower quality of that individual plant.*

WHERE TO BUY ORCHIDS   The orchid business is a large and growing one. There are orchid growers in practically every part of our country. Prices of different types of orchids vary greatly, but the prices of the same types of orchid are very nearly equal all over the country. In the orchid business, as in any other, you get what you pay for.

When you buy plants from a legitimate and well-established orchid grower, the price you pay includes a great deal more than the plant alone. You are paying also for service, integrity and guarantee. Legitimate orchid growers want to help you with your problems. They take a real interest in your progress and success and are always willing to supply advice and information on any questions or problems you may have. This is only part of the service that you should get from legitimate growers. Another part of their service is careful packing and shipping of your plants to insure safe delivery.

Integrity and guarantee are the basis of all sound business. Legitimate growers stand by all sales. They should guarantee plants to be as represented; to be healthy, to be suitable for hobby growing; to arrive safely so that the hobbyist has a good chance of success.

The orchid business, like any other, has its cut-rate dealers. These are usually brokers, not growers. They buy and sell wherever they can find plants at the right price for rapid turnover. To insure these rapid sales, they must sell at cheaper prices than the established concerns. This usually means that the plants they are selling are inferior stock—often culls which the legitimate grower is unwilling to sell under his own name. Such dealers are generally either incapable of supplying or unwilling to supply the service, integrity, and guarantees on which legitimate growers base their whole reputations. These dealers depend on advertising to attract the beginner. They usually are advertising the same named plants but at "bargain" prices. The beginner will do well to beware of such "bargains." Just as all people named Smith are not of the same worth or all boxer dogs of the same value, so all orchids of the same name are not of equal value. Orchid plants, like people or dogs, are individuals, and as individuals they vary greatly from each other. Thus it is often possible to buy plants of the same name at prices ranging from as little as $5.00 to as much as $100.00. You may be sure the quality of these plants and flowers will show the same variation as the price. In short, you will get what you pay for—the legitimate grower will stand by his sales and replace stock that does not measure up to the quality advertised.

ACTUAL BARGAINS   Occasionally you will find true bargains. As in other businesses, legitimate growers sometimes have sales. A grower may become overstocked with one particular type of orchid; perhaps he becomes cramped for space or does a housecleaning job, replacing plants which bloom at the wrong season for him, plants that grow so big that they take up too much room or perhaps produce flowers that for some insignificant reason are not popular with florists. A commercial man cannot afford to grow such plants, but for the amateur these would be perfectly suitable and desirable. Also occasionally a grower goes out of business or a hobbyist will give up his hobby for some reason. Under such conditions actual bargains are possible.

Several legitimate growers around the country have very attractive bargains in the form of introductory offers to get interested people started on their hobby. For some years now the Fennell Orchid Company, Homestead, Florida, has been running several of these introductory offers. These are collections of plants suitable for the amateur to grow and selected to give bloom around the year. These starter collections range in price from $11.00 to $128.50 and are actually priced at about two thirds of the combined value of the plants. Other growers around the country also follow this policy, and such collections are true bargains.

SEEDLINGS In many ways unflowered seedlings are the best buy in the orchid world. When you buy seedlings from legitimate growers, you can get the newest crosses from the finest stud plants available today. When they bloom, your plants will be new and modern-type hybrids. If these seedlings are bought in smaller sizes, they are very inexpensive. The most economical sizes are those plants just out of community pots and planted in individual containers from 1¾-inch to 3-inch pot size. Plants that are from 2 inches to 4 inches tall and established in individual pots are over the danger period of their early life and will, with normal care, grow to bloom within two to four years. This is the smallest really safe size for the beginner to tackle. Such plants sell for $1.50 to $3.50 each, depending on quality and the quantity purchased. The price increases rapidly as the plants get bigger because they take up more room and require more individual care, both of which are expensive to the commercial grower. When these plants bloom, most of them will be of a quality which would cost $25 apiece and up if bought in bloom. Thus for the investment of $1.50 to $3.50 and two to four years of your time, you are returned plants of $25 value. After all, time is cheap as a hobby, and there is something fascinating and rewarding about growing your own plants to maturity.

There are two drawbacks with these seedlings. First of all, the two- to four-year wait for the flowers is likely to discourage the beginner, and it is definitely better to start with a few mature plants first. Learn on these plants and, as they bloom, they will keep your interest going. Then, after you know a little about orchid culture and are beginning to feel more sure of your ability, you can start on seedlings. Actually seedlings are not any harder to grow than the mature plants, but being small, they have less resistance to the mistakes of the beginner and are more likely to be set back or stunted during the learning period. The other drawback which must be taken into account is that seedlings do vary as individuals, just like brothers and sisters in a family. They won't all look alike, and you can't tell exactly what they will look like until they bloom. However, just as in people—and the percentages are about the same—if you breed from two very attractive parents, you are quite likely to get very attractive children. You can even predict that the children will have many of the same characteristics as the parents; you can hope that some of them at least will possess a happy mixture of the better characteristics of both parents. More than this you cannot do. How many of them will turn out in any one particular way is impossible to tell until the first flowers are produced.

RULES FOR ORCHID BUYING

1. Buy from established, reputable firms who will stand by their plants.
2. Select strong, healthy plants with live roots, already established in their pots.
3. Start with mature plants; don't try seedlings until you know something about growing orchids.
4. Beware of "bargains"—remember, you get what you pay for.

What Is An Orchid Worth? *

What does a sunset cost? Can you hold a symphony in your hand? Perhaps you pay ten dollars for an opera seat. It's not too high because you get full measure of joy from it.

Have you ever sat quietly, for ten minutes, say, contemplating an orchid bloom? Try it. You'll have a pleasant

* *By D. B. Fennell reprinted from Fennell's* Orchid News, *Vol. 8, No. 1, 1954.*

surprise. The beauty grows on you. Think of the years it took to grow this plant from tiny seed—the care to pack and ship it—its guaranteed safe arrival. Many people have labored to bring it to you.

Think what the beauty of an orchid means to you—that this plant will never die of old age.

What is an orchid worth? That's for you to decide. We say it's worth the pleasure you get from it.

chapter 5

Starting Your Collection

There are several points to consider once you decide to start growing your own orchids.

1. Start with mature plants which will give you immediate satisfaction.

2. Start small with a few plants. Add to your collection as you learn more about the plants. Beginning with a lot of plants at once is liable to be overwhelming. The problems that can come up may scare you off before you get well started. With a few plants problems arise one at a time and can be met as they come up without undue alarm.

3. Start with *Cattleyas*, the big fancy corsage-type flower that everyone knows. It is not only the most thrilling to the beginner, but it is also the toughest and the most tolerant of orchid plants and the easiest to grow under home conditions.

4. Plan for year-round bloom as you buy your plants. This gives continual satisfaction without long waits between flowers.

5. Buy only a few plants of any one type. Try to get as many different types as possible. Variety is the spice of orchid growing.

6. Make sure the plants you select are suitable for your conditions—of sun and temperature particularly.

7. If you don't see the plants in bloom, ask for details of quality. Don't buy by name alone.

8. Know the dealers you're buying from, whether they stand by their sales, will help you with your problems, supply the information that you need, et cetera.

chapter 6

Beginner's Collections

No. 1—BASIC COLLECTION *   This collection will give year-round bloom, and it also will supply some variety of sizes and colors.

WINTER

C. Trianae	light lavender corsage-type	Nov.-Feb.	$8.50
Phal. Doris	white spray-type	winter and spring	8.50

SPRING

C. Skinneri	dark lavender cluster-type	Mar.-Apr.	8.50
C. Mossiae	dark lavender heavy bloomer corsage-type	Apr.-May	10.00

SUMMER

C. Gaskelliana	lavender corsage-type	May-July	8.50
C. Bowringiana	dark lavender cluster-type	Aug.-Sept.	8.50

FALL

Den. Phalae-nopsis	lavender spray-type	Sept.-Nov.	6.00-15.00
L. Anceps	lavender spray-type	Oct.-Dec.	5.00-10.00
	Cost of whole group about		$63.50

* *Several such collections are offered by the Fennell Orchid Company, Homestead, Florida. They have been set up to give the hobbyist "Starter Collections" at prices of $25.00 and up.*

This is a collection to start with, a solid basis to add to as you go along. All these plants are readily available and inexpensive. The prices quoted are general. They are given only as an indication of the average price. You should be able to get healthy, strong, blooming-size plants of average quality at close to these prices almost anywhere around the country. It should be possible to purchase this whole collection for about $63.50. If you figure that the individual flowers will last approximately three weeks each as a bare minimum, then the eight plants listed will supply you with flowers twenty-four weeks out of the year, or about half the time off and on the year round. You can add to this basic collection as you can afford it or as some particular plant catches your eye. The best way is to add to your basic collection systematically. Plan to fill in the bloomless spaces to insure more constant year-round bloom. The surest way to do this is to buy plants in bloom or in bud when none of your others are in flower. Your plants will bloom in very much the same order year after year. Weather conditions may make them bloom somewhat earlier or later than normal, but the same conditions will affect most of the plants approximately the same way so that the order of blooming will remain quite constant. Thus it really is possible to plan your collection for continual bloom with a minimum of plants.

PLAN YOUR COLLECTION!   Once you have acquired your basic collection and have learned enough about the plants to feel sure of your growing ability, it is a good time to decide exactly what kind of a collection you are aiming for. Different collectors are particularly interested in different types of orchids, and the more you learn about the plants, the more likely you are to become interested in one particular type of collection. All too often hobbyists allow their collections to just grow "like Topsy," and if you can settle on some particular goal, you will save yourself a great many disappointments resulting from haphazard buying.

There are many possible kinds of orchid collections. Some people are interested only in plants of highest flower quality; others want the greatest possible variety. Many people are interested only in the large-flowered types. The most avid collectors seem to specialize in botanical orchids, a field which is in many ways the most challenging of all as the possibilities are almost unlimited.

At this time it is also well to decide how you intend to build your collection—whether you plan to limit yourself to mature plants only or whether you plan to add to the basic group mainly with seedlings. Any such plan will make it much easier for you when the time comes to buy additional plants.

Since most amateurs are primarily interested in large-flowered types at first, the second suggested collection is:

No. 2—THE MATURE HYBRID COLLECTION For the hobbyist who can afford it, such a group could be used as a beginner's basic collection, supplying a generally higher quality of flower than Collection No. 1, but this selection is primarily intended as a follow-up, an addition to Collection No. 1. After the hobbyist has grown orchids for a while and knows something about them, he usually becomes interested in the finer types which he wasn't willing to pay for until he knew more about growing the plants. This collection will give a high quality of flowers, more variety of color and season, and many of the plants listed will bloom more than once a year when growing steadily. There are so many different hybrids that you can buy individuals of any of these types which will bloom any season you prefer.

> Pure white *Cattleya* hybrid
> White with purple lip *Cattleya* hybrid
> Blc—large with frilly lip
> Lc hybrid—dark
> White Bc hybrid—with frilly lip
> Dark *Cattleya* hybrid

No. 3—"SOON-TO-BLOOM" HYBRID COLLECTION A collection of much the same type plants as those in Collection No. 2, but made up of seedlings about two-thirds grown, which will bloom in a year to eighteen months. Such a collection gives the variety and quality of Collection No. 2 but is much less expensive. Of course the plants are smaller, and the flowers will be smaller the first year or two of blooming.

No. 4—SEEDLING COLLECTION   The best way to build up a fine collection at the least expense is with seedling collections. Buy small 1½- to 2-year-old seedlings, which can give quality, variety and year-round bloom at the least expense with a wait of only two to four years.

No. 5—VARIETY COLLECTION   (Botanicals for your collection) There are many unusual orchids that are easy to grow and easy to acquire. They add variety and spice to your collection, and many growers fall in love with these types to the exclusion of *Cattleyas*.

Most of the plants listed in Chapter 3, the parts on *Dendrobiums*, *Phalaenopsis*, *Vandas* and *Botanicals* are easy to grow and are readily available on the market. They come in all colors, sizes, shapes and seasons, with price ranges from $5.00 and up. They will provide never-failing interest, enjoyment and an endless quest for the collector.

chapter 7

Dividing and Repotting

This is the only real work in orchid growing, and it is very important that it be done right. The strength and future growth of your plants depend a great deal on the job of dividing and repotting that you do. Luckily, repotting is not needed often, and actually, it should not be done unless absolutely necessary: *Orchid plants do not like to be disturbed at their roots.*

There are two reasons why a plant should be repotted:

1. When the plant grows so that the bulbs themselves, not just the roots, have grown out over the edge of the pot, then it is time to repot. (*See* Fig. 17)

2. Also if the potting material should become rotten before the plant has grown out of the pot, the plant should be repotted anyway, because rotten potting material becomes a great deal like soil—packing down, clogging up drainage, and staying much too wet, resulting in root rot and very weak plants.

Before repotting an orchid, make sure that it really needs it. The biggest mistake commonly made by beginners is the too-frequent dividing and repotting of plants. They will do much better if you will leave them alone until they really need repotting. If you are sure that they really do, the process is actually quite simple. Most important is that the plants should be repotted at the *right stage of growth.*

There are two stages of growth which are best for repotting. The *best* time of all is *just as the plant starts its new roots.* By careful observation you will notice the new roots starting to come out of the rhizome at the front of the plant, and this is by far the best time to repot because the plant roots into the new potting material immediately with the smallest possible amount of lost time. The *next best time* to repot a plant is *immediately after blooming*. The plant is likely to be more or less dormant for a short while at this stage, and repotting will not disturb it seriously.

17.   ORCHID PLANT GROWING OUT OF THE POT.

The first thing to do is to take the plant out of its pot, being careful to disturb the roots as little as possible.

1.   Run a knife blade around under the roots outside of the pot, loosening them, and then repeat on the inside lip of the pot.

2.   Use a strong knife blade or screw driver to pry the plant upwards and out of the pot.

3.   Carefully remove the rotted potting material and dead roots, leaving all live roots and any still fresh potting material that is still good; there is no reason to disturb the roots unnecessarily while removing it.

4. At this point you should decide whether or not you are going to divide the plant. Most people divide their plants much too often. Keeping them small and dividing at every opportunity gives you more plants, it is true, but many less flowers and a great deal more work. It actually comes down to deciding whether you want lots of plants or lots of flowers. If you need plants for sale, trade or gifts, then dividing them often and keeping them small will pay off. If you want the most flowers possible for your greatest enjoyment—plants that are really showy—then don't divide them. Leave them big and repot into a larger pot. Bigger plants put out stronger growths and more of them than the small divisions. Naturally this results in more flowers, too. Plants that are left big and placed in larger pots grow much more quickly than smaller divisions, and specimen plants can be produced in only a few years by this process. These larger plants increase in size like a snowball rolling down hill; the bigger they are, the faster they grow, and the bigger they get. The art of growing specimen plants has been neglected in recent years, and it is a shame because actually it is very rewarding. Nothing is more thrilling than producing a truly large specimen plant literally covered with blooms. The hobby grower has a definite edge on the professional in this field of orchid growing because the professional must divide his plants in order to have smaller ones for sale. Specimen plants are a sign of a real grower.

Sometimes it is advisable to divide your plants. There are three common situations in which dividing is called for:

1. Most common is when a plant grows along as a single or unbranching rhizome (Fig. 18, a). Such a plant soon requires a large pot and yet continues to produce flowers on only one stem at a time (Fig. 18, b). These plants look ungainly and do not grow well in the larger size pots so that it is best to divide them (Fig. 18, c), keeping only the front four or five bulbs to repot and cutting off and discarding the back bulbs (Fig. 18, d). If the back bulbs are particularly strong and have a good set of roots, it may be worthwhile to pot them up too (Fig. 18, e), but usually they take so long to produce blooms that they are seldom worth fooling with.

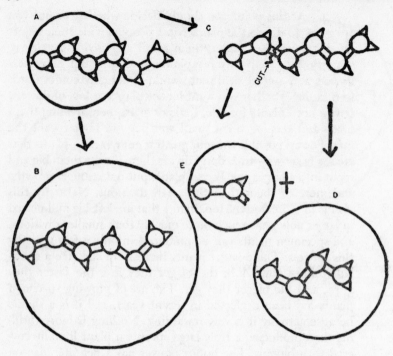

18.   Dividing a Single or Unbranched Plant.

2.   Specimen plants will finally become too large to handle easily. We seldom grow plants on after they need repotting into containers larger than the 10- to 12-inch sizes. A plant that is too big for 10- to 12-inch pots is really very awkward to handle, and for the sake of practicality can best be divided into two or three large plants.

3.   Occasionally a large plant will start branching so profusely that the rhizomes crisscross and soon produce a hopeless tangle. Once a plant starts this, it seldom continues growing strongly. It becomes so crowded that the resulting growth is usually weedy and weak. Also the rhizomes which are buried underneath the crisscrossing rhizomes quite often rot, and under such crowded conditions the rot often goes undetected until the whole plant is infected. Therefore, it is

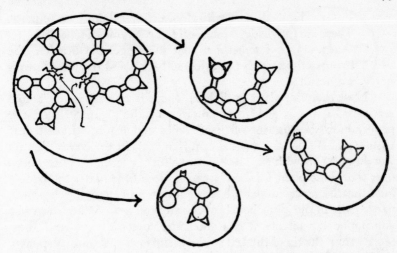

19. Dividing a Specimen Plant Large branched plants sometimes become too big to repot as one plant. These should be divided and repotted. In this case one could get 3 plants each with front leads with a minimum of 4 bulbs each. Note: plants should be placed carefully in pots to use smallest size with most growing room in front of new leads.

usually advisable to repot and divide such a plant as soon as this crisscrossing starts. Careful dividing can produce two or three large plants, and it is seldom necessary to reduce to small divisions. Sometimes it is possible in this situation to merely cut out one or two of the branching leads, like careful pruning of a tree, so that you give the main plant more growing room. In this manner the large plant can be kept almost intact.

If you must divide, there are a few simple rules to follow:

1. Keep a blooming size division, never less than four bulbs with a front lead, on *Cattleyas*. If you can keep larger plants of several leads, they will do even better.

2. Try to get divisions with good root systems—live roots along part of the rhizome at least.

3. Cut the rhizome with a sharp blade; never use scissors, shears or clippers which crush the tissue and make fungus or bacterial infections more likely.

4. Dust all cuts with "flowers of sulphur" or fermate. These are fungicides which seal the cut from infection.

5. Always remember that the bigger the division, the stronger the growth (with less setback), and the more flowers will result.

Now that the plant is divided, there is one more job before repotting. This is a good time to clean up the plant. Strip off the papery bulb sheaths, cut off dead bulbs and leaves, withered leaf tissues; and cut out any injured or rotten spots in the leaves. Be sure you dust all cuts with the "flowers of sulfur" or fermate. Then check over the whole plant for insects which often hide under the papery bulb sheaths, on the underside of the leaves, and along the rhizomes, particularly in the joints between rhizome and bulb. Whether or not you notice any insects, it is a good idea to scrub the plants thoroughly from the tip of the leaf to the rhizome at this time. A sponge, cloth, or soft brush is good for this job. Use any bland soap, such as Ivory, and tepid water. Scrub especially well the undersides of the leaves, the joint of leaf and bulb, in the bulb grooves, the joint of bulb and rhizome, and along the rhizome. An old toothbrush is particularly good for scrubbing the joints of bulbs and leaves and bulbs and the rhizome. After scrubbing, the plant can be dipped in a good plant spray. Leaves, bulbs, roots and all should be completely immersed. This is not necessary, but it helps to prevent any possible insect trouble. If you have so many plants that scrubbing becomes a chore, then you definitely should dip all plants in place of scrubbing.

At last you are ready to pot. The actual process is very simple, but there are several definite requirements:

1. The *container and material must supply good drainage and ventilation* so that the roots can dry out quickly and completely after watering.

Container   Special pots are now being made for orchids. They have slits cut into the sides for better ventilation and more complete drainage. Shallow pots, such as azalea pots, and bulb pans are most satisfactory in the larger sizes as orchids do not put out many roots and often do not fill a large, deep pot.

Material   Osmunda fiber, a coarse, black fiber (the roots of a fern) is the traditional potting material for most orchids. In the last few years, however, a revolution in the methods and materials of orchid potting has taken place. A great deal of experimental work has been done in search of an easier-to-use and less expensive potting material than the osmunda fiber and many growers are now using granulated tree barks instead of osmunda fiber.

The bark from almost any of the coniferous trees seems to be all right but Pine bark and Fir bark are the two being used most. These barks come in a variety of sizes and grades. In general, sizes should be varied to fit with pot sizes. The larger pot used, the larger size of bark should be used with it. Little or no fine particles should be left in any of the grades, as the roots need good drainage and ventilation. Potting with bark has several advantages:

    a.   Much easier to use—pots just like soil.

    b.   Somewhat less expensive.

    c.   Much quicker.

    d.   Not as subject to overwatering.

There are several disadvantages too:

    a.   You must feed and much more heavily.

    b.   You must water more.

    c.   This is a new potting material. Not enough is known about it yet. Its use is still experimental and recommendations for growing in it are subject to change at any time.

    d.   There is a type of white-cottony fungus that sometimes attacks the bark. Doesn't seem to hurt the orchids, except that it sheds water and makes it very hard to water the bark properly. A little detergent in the water makes it penetrate better.

The big advantage to the use of bark for orchid potting is best pointed out by the slogan of one of the bark suppliers: "If you aren't potting with bark, you're working too hard!" See for yourself. Compare the step-by-step potting instructions for Osmunda and Bark.

Drainage   You will also need a supply of pieces of broken pot, chunks of charcoal, or large gravel for drainage in the bottom of the pot.

    2.   Undoubtedly the most important requirement of orchid potting is that the *plants must be potted so tightly that they are held firmly in place, and the rhizomes and roots of the plant cannot wiggle or move in the potting material.*

The new root tips are very soft and tender, almost jelly-like and will be broken off and killed if the plant moves while the new roots are entering the fiber or bark.

3.   Plants should be repotted with *only enough growing room for two or three years*. The potting material will last only about this long before rotting, and it is uneconomical to allow the plants more room than they need. A plant should be placed in the pot in a position which gives *the most growing room at the front of the plant with the least waste space at the sides or back*. If the rhizome is relatively straight, the back end of it should be placed against one edge of the pot with the plant pointing straight across the pot so that there is as much room as possible between the front of the plant

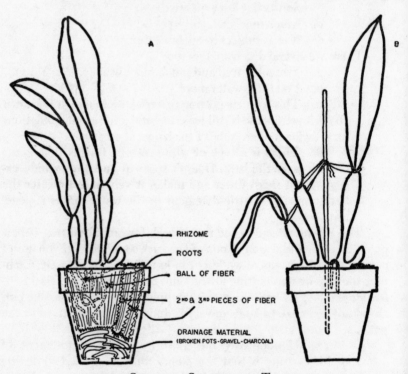

RHIZOME

ROOTS

BALL OF FIBER

2ᴺᴰ & 3ᴿᴰ PIECES OF FIBER

DRAINAGE MATERIAL
(BROKEN POTS-GRAVEL-CHARCOAL)

20.   STAPLING, STAKING AND TYPING.

and the other side of the pot. Usually you should allow two or three times the distance between the bulbs in front of the new lead. This usually amounts to about two inches on Cattleyas.

4. The *rhizomes should be buried* only about *halfway into the potting material* with the upper half exposed. If the rhizome is buried completely under the surface of the potting material, it will rot. If the plant is planted so that the rhizome and some of the roots are completely exposed to the air, the plant will never root into the potting material satisfactorily.

5. The *top level of the potting material should be kept even with the rim of the pot.* This is the easiest, best looking, and safest way to pot.

6. If the plant does not have a good root system to anchor it when repotted, and hold it until the new roots come out, then it should be *staked and tied to keep it from wiggling* while rooting. Sometimes it is advisable also to staple down the rhizome to hold it firmly in place until the new roots are formed. Staking and tying is also done for the sake of appearance and to avoid sprawling. Plants tied up to a stake look much neater and take up less room.

STEP-BY-STEP POTTING METHOD IN OSMUNDA FIBER

1. Select correct size pot. If possible, one with slits. Fill about one quarter full of drainage material (broken pots, gravel or charcoal). If you choose a regular flower pot, fill it about one-third to one-half full of drainage material.

2. Hold plant in left hand. Build up a ball of fiber in and around roots of the plant. Keep the back end of the rhizome at the edge of the ball with the rhizome itself running along the top of the ball, half in and half out of the fiber. Build forward along the rhizome and out in front of the lead until the ball is about the size of the pot.

3. Place plant and ball of fiber in the pot. Hold plant in place with the left hand, keeping the back end of the rhizome firmly against the edge of the pot. The front end or lead of the plant should be held pointing toward the farthest

point of the pot rim. Now push the fiber back toward the back of the plant, making room between the front of the ball and the rim of the pot.

4. Add more fiber until very tight. Use large pieces of fiber, running from the top to the bottom of the pot in a vertical fashion. Do not fill pot with horizontal layers of fiber because it is very hard to get the fiber really tight in this manner. Keep adding fiber always between the existing fiber and the front rim of the pot. This constantly pushes the plant and fiber backwards so that the back end of the rhizome stays against the edge of the pot without leaving waste space. Be careful during this process to keep from burying the rhizome or allowing it to raise up out of the fiber. Also be careful not to allow the fiber to mount up in the center of the pot. These difficulties are very likely to come up when you are first learning to pot. The only remedy is to pull out some of the fiber and start over again, keeping the rhizome and fiber level with the rim of the pot. A large screw driver, the point of your garden shears, or a sharpened stick will be quite useful in the last stage of cramming fiber into the pot. You should get as much fiber as possible into the pot so that it is really hard and tight.

5. Test for wiggling. Shake the pot. The leaves will move, but the *rhizome should not*. If the rhizome does move, then staple it down and stake it. Tie the leaves until the rhizome cannot move when the pot is shaken. (See Fig. 20, B)

6. Test for tightness. You should be able to lift the plant, pot and all, by the leaves, and shake it without the pot falling off.

7. For the sake of appearance, trim the fiber even to the level of the pot.

CARE OF PLANT AFTER REPOTTING IN OSMUNDA

This repotting and dividing is, of course, somewhat of a shock to the plant, mostly because of the loss of roots and damage to the roots during repotting. Naturally, any injury of the roots of the plant lessens its ability to pick up water and food. Plants repotted at the right stage of growth will have little or no setback, but you must expect some shriveling of the leaves after repotting.

Watering   The most important part of the care of your plant after repotting concerns watering. You should *keep* newly repotted plants *somewhat on the dry side*. Their roots cannot pick up much water anyway, and this dryness will induce the plant to put out new root growth quickly. Occasional light waterings, only about one half as often as usual, are all that is necessary. Sprinkling the leaves lightly every day will help reduce shriveling until the new roots come out. As soon as the new roots appear from the rhizome and start out into the fiber, you may resume your normal watering and feeding schedule, and all shriveling should disappear soon thereafter.

REPOTTING IN BARK
Preparation of the Bark   Before potting, the bark should be treated as follows: Screen out or shake out the accumulation of fine particles and dust. Save this for tiny seedlings or throw it away. Then soak the bark overnight or for a couple of hours in a solution of 1 teaspoonful of Ammonium nitrate and one-quarter teaspoon of household detergent such as Joy or Dreft (do not use any that contain Chlorine) to each gallon of water. This gives the plants a better start and makes the bark easier to water at first. Then drain the bark and pot. Damp bark is much easier and more pleasant to pot with. Soaking keeps down the dust and makes it easier on your hands as well.

Preparation of Plant   If plant has been in osmunda fiber, *all fiber must be removed before potting into bark*. Old fiber and old roots should be stripped off completely leaving only strong and turgid roots. If plant has a heavy root system, much of it can be trimmed off too. Leave only enough roots to form a good anchor for the plant when repotted.

If plant has previously been in bark, it is all right to leave on any bark that the roots hold tightly, but it is best to shake out any small stuff or any bark that has rotted and become soft. Old dead roots should also be removed before repotting.

STEP-BY-STEP POTTING METHOD—BARK

1. Select correct size pot. If possible, one with slits. Fill about one-quarter full of drainage material (broken pots, gravel or charcoal). If you choose a regular flower pot, fill it about one-third to one-half full of drainage material.

2. Hold plant in place in the pot with your left hand. Keep the back end of the rhizome against one edge of the pot with the front end pointing out across the pot in the direction which gives the most growing room between front bulb and far side of the pot.

3. Pot as with soil. Use right hand to fill in the pot with bark. After each handful tamp down the bark with fingers or a blunt stick. Don't wait until pot is full to try and tamp the bark.

4. When pot is full lift it and tap it sharply on table two or three times to settle bark tightly. Then fill in to lip of pot with more bark if necessary.

5. Since it is not possible to pack bark tightly enough to hold plant really firmly until it roots, it is best to use a wire clip to hold the rhizome down. A straight piece of heavy wire cut just barely longer than the inside diameter of the pot, laid across the rhizome and then pushed down firmly at either end until rhizome is held down and ends of wire wedge in tightly against pot sides will hold the plant securely. Special pot clips are also made for this purpose. These clip onto rim of the pot with a prong that reaches out part way across the pot and holds down the rhizome. These pot clips have the advantage that they can be put onto the pot anywhere around the rim for best pressure on the rhizome.

6. Now stake up the plant for a neat appearance. Straight stakes down into the bark do not hold the plant firmly as the bark is too loose. Special clip-on stakes are made which clip onto the pot rim. These give much better support for plants potted in bark. Plants are tied to these stakes in the conventional manner or Clip-on Ring Stakes, which have a ring at the top, can be used to hold the leaves up and in. These ring stakes do away with tying with string and give a neater appearance. They are also safer as there are no narrow

Modern strap-leaved Vanda hybrids — Left, Vanda Chimy Walker, center, Vanda Carol Hirano and right, a fine blue variety of Vanda Chimy Walker.

TOP LEFT: One of the lovely guides at the Orchid Jungle showing the rare and exotic Scorpion Orchid — *Arachnis Moschifera*

TOP RIGHT: *Angraecum Sesquipedale* — the tail is up to 18" long

BOTTOM: Specimen plant of *C. trianaei* variety Mary Fennell

Top: *Catasetum species* — yellow spotted red
Bottom left: *Calanthe* William Murray
Bottom right: *Lycaste Aromatica*

GROUP OF UNUSUAL ORCHIDS

TOP LEFT: *Epidendrum alatum* — 2½" flowers, very rare
TOP CENTER: *Brassia longissima* — Very striking flowers
— 8-10"— long, fine and rare
TOP RIGHT: *Epidendrum Atropurpureum* — Very exotic
bloom
BOTTOM CENTER: *Brassia caudata* — Rare, very spidery 5"
flowers
BOTTOM RIGHT: *Epidendrum Howardii* — 1" flower, very
dainty, called "bright eyes"

loops of string to entangle and choke new growths as they grow upwards.

CARE OF PLANT AFTER REPOTTING IN BARK

Something about bark seems to act as a stimulant to root growth. New roots will start to form almost immediately after repotting. Humidity should be kept high after repotting and watering can be resumed on a normal schedule immediately after repotting. There is no need, nor is it even advisable, to keep the plants on the dry side after bark potting. *This is quite different from culture in osmunda and should be noted.*

Remember—barks supply almost no food to the plant. Therefore, you must feed regularly and heavily if you expect your plants to grow and bloom properly. Feed with extra nitrogen, too. Use Fenorco Plant Food on every other watering and use Ammonium nitrate with the in-between waterings, both at the rate of 1 teaspoonful to 1 gallon of water.

The change-over from osmunda to bark is sometimes a shock to the plant, especially if watering and feeding are not watched carefully and given consistently. Back leaves on the plants may yellow somewhat but should soon recover if feeding is increased slightly and done regularly.

chapter 8

Insects and Diseases

Luckily, there are very few insects and diseases that are likely to trouble your orchids. Actually, they are seldom serious and are generally easy to combat. Orchids in home culture are seldom exposed to either insects or diseases.

INSECTS   Most garden insects occasionally bother orchids, but the plants are tough, and the insects usually prefer other more tender garden plants. There are only three insects that are commonly found on orchids:

Scale is the most common and the most serious. There are many types of scale, but one in particular seems to like orchid plants. This is the Bois Duval or "white cottony scale." It is quite easy to recognize. The female is round and flat, something like an oyster on the half shell, and varies from one sixteenth of an inch to one eighth of an inch in diameter. Its color is grayish white. The male is a cottony, fuzzy, rodlike creature about one sixteenth of an inch long and half as wide. It looks like a miniature pipe cleaner. These insects often form whole colonies or clusters, piling up on each other and completely covering whole sections of the plant. They harm the plant by sucking the juices from it. Over a long period bad infestations can seriously weaken or even kill the plant. They are usually found in hidden places—on the underside of leaves, under bulb sheaths, at the joint of leaf and bulb, around the base of the flower sheath, on the rhizome, and at the joint of bulb and rhizome.

Control: The easiest, safest, and most complete way to get rid of scale is to strip down all of the bulb sheaths and scrub the

whole plant with a soft brush, soap and water. An old toothbrush is ideal for the job, and any bland soap, such as Ivory, will
do. The whole plant should be scrubbed, as the immature stages
of the scale are not readily visible to the naked eye. If you have
too many plants to scrub, you can kill scale by spraying with
DDT in an oil emulsion. Parathion and Malathon are also very
good for killing scale, but great care must be used with these
sprays as they can kill you, too. All recommended precautions
should be taken, and actually it would be safer to leave them
alone. Spraying should be done once every two weeks for three
times, as none of these sprays kill the adults; only the young
crawling stages are killed, but the adults will die off of old age
in the six-week period.

The Fennell Orchid Co. of Homestead, Florida, manufactures an Oil Emulsion DDT spray which was especially developed for Orchids by Dr. Ernest Cory of the University of
Maryland. FENORCO PLANT SPRAY is especially effective
for the control of scale.

Red Spider is quite common but hard to spot because it is not
readily visible to the naked eye. Red-spider damage, however, is
visible and quite easy to identify. This tiny insect works on the
underside of the leaf, causing yellowish or whitish spots and
blotches approximately the size of a pencil eraser on the top of
the leaf. If you notice such spots and splotches, careful inspec-
tion of the underside of the leaf will show very light yellowish
brown, rusty-looking spots about one sixteenth of an inch in
diameter in the center of slightly sunken yellowish areas. This
is the web of the spider, and a strong magnifying glass will show
a small green or brownish insect in the center of the reddish
web. Actually, red spider is not a spider; it belongs to the mite
family. Red spider is a sucking insect, and it thrives under dry
conditions. It is usually found on new growths or on soft, suc-
culent-leaved types of orchids. Occasionally it is found even on
tough mature Cattleya leaves. Large and widespread infestations of red spider often have a grayish silvery sheen. The whole
leaf or the infested part will be silvery in appearance.

Control: Best control is scrubbing, followed by dusting, with
flowers of sulfur or spraying with a miticide. There are several

good miticides on the market. Dimite and Kelthane are two of these. If it is practical to do so, raising the humidity will also help control this insect. DDT, Parathion and Malathon are not effective on red spider.

Slugs are snails without shells. There are two types commonly found on orchids. The large ones are flat, slimy creatures, approximately ½ to ¾ of an inch wide and 1½ to 3 inches long. The small ones are about ⅛ of an inch in diameter and about ½ to ¾ of an inch long. This is a chewing pest which feeds on flowers, buds, new growths and soft leaves and roots. They are often hard to find because they work mainly at night. It is easy to recognize their damage, however, by the tracks of slimy, shiny mucus that they leave behind them as they crawl along. They usually hide in or under the pots during the daytime.

Control: Hand pick at night as the slugs work or spray or dust the plant, pot, benches et cetera, with Metaldehyde slug poison. This is on the market in several forms. California Chemical Company has a spray containing Metaldehyde. Metaldehyde is also sold in the form of pellets for slug baits, but this has not proved too effective in our experience, especially in large areas. DDT, Malathon and Parathion are not effective on slugs. Most effective control is obtained with regular sprayings of plants, pots, benches, walls and ground of growing area with "NEW IMPROVED FENORCO," a Plant Spray containing Metaldehyde, manufactured by The Fennell Orchid Company of Homestead, Florida.

CAUTION: Metaldehyde, in large quantities, is poisonous if eaten by children and pets. Keep it out of the way. Baits are particularly attractive and dangerous to children and pets. Spraying is not dangerous as they would have to lick a large area in order to get enough poison to harm them.

Other Insects are occasionally found on orchids; scrubbing them off is the surest control. Spraying with DDT, Chlorodane, Metaldehyde, Parathion and Malathon are the only practical controls for insects in general on larger collections.

It is a good idea to either scrub or spray regularly. A schedule of every month to six weeks the year round is advisable, whether or not any insects are noticed. An ounce of prevention is worth a pound of cure. It is much easier to keep insects out than to get rid of them.

Most common garden sprays available from local Garden Supply Stores can be used on orchids if directions are followed carefully. In general it is safest to use these at the lower recommended strength. However, to control all insects, you will need a whole shelfful of these sprays. The Fennell Orchid Company of Homestead, Florida, now produces a new "all-purpose" spray for orchids, which controls almost all orchid pests. This "New Improved Fenorco Plant Spray" does the whole job in one operation and saves much work and time. This spray contains DDT, Chlorodane, Dimite and Metaldehyde and is much safer for you to use than some of the other new insecticides.

DISEASES   Orchid diseases are few and far between. There are three general types, and actually, very little is known about any of them.

Fungus and bacteria   Most common are the fungus and bacteria infections. These are usually the result of overwatering and too high humidity. Very little scientific work has been done on these until recently, and not much is known about them even yet. Undoubtedly, there are several types of both fungi and bacteria found in orchids. They usually take the form of rot in the bulbs, leaves and rhizomes.

Fungus shows up most often in new growths, starting either in the tip, which blackens and dies, and working backwards down the leaf of the plant, or starting in the cup formed by the opening new leaf, in which case the whole new growth turns black and dies. Both of these forms can progress backwards through the rhizome and eventually cause the death of the whole plant. In both cases the plant tissue turns black, feels oily and wet, much softer than normal tissue. This is usually called "Black-Rot" and is caused by too much water, high humidity, or water standing overnight in the cup of the new growth.

Control: The only sure control is to cut off all infected parts. Cut well below the black rot into the clear, healthy green tissue. If more than one cut is necessary, sterilize the knife between cuts; flaming it with a match will do the job. Dust cut edges with "flowers of sulphur" or Fermate. This will seal the cut from further infection.

Bacteria—This is another type of rot which is much more drastic as it acts more quickly. The infected area turns grayish green and almost translucent, feels soft and greasy to the touch. It looks as if it had been soaked in oil and is very limp like the lettuce in yesterday's salad. This infection sweeps through the plants in a matter of one or two days, and, unfortunately, is seldom noticed before it is too late. Luckily, it is rare and chances are you will never be confronted with it.

Control: If you notice bacteria rot before the whole plant is infected, cut off the infected part, making your cut at least 1½ to 2 inches below the infection. Dust the cut area with fermate or "flowers of sulfur," and be sure to sterilize your knife after every cut and after the job is finished. Don't take chances on spreading the infection with the knife. If the infection seems to be throughout the whole plant, burn it to keep the infection from spreading, and sterilize the pot before re-using.

These rots usually occur in very rainy, wet periods, when the humidity is high. Luckily, none are very common, and prevention is usually easy. Be observant. Quickly cut out and destroy infected parts or whole plants. If you watch your plants carefully, you can keep rot from spreading. If any of these rots show up in more than one or two separated cases, it is a good idea to spray all of your plants with a good fungicide. Fungicides and bactericides are usually effective only on certain types of fungus or bacteria. Thus to control fungi or bacteria in general, it is advisable to use several different compounds. Sometimes you will have to try several before you find the one that controls the particular fungus or bacteria causing your trouble. Some of the most popular of these for use on orchids are Captan, Fermate, Parzate, Tersan and Wilson's Anti-Damp. Recently some of the anti-biotics have also been used to good effect on orchids. Two of these are Agri-mycin and Agri-strep.

Virus—This is the other type of orchid disease which is found occasionally; it is usually called "the orchid virus disease" for lack of information and a better name. Actually, almost nothing is known about this disease. Some growers feel that there are several kinds of virus diseases in orchids, and some scientific

21. SHOWING THE DIFFERENCE BETWEEN BLACK-ROT AND SUNBURN.
Left—Black Rot   Right—Sunburn

Differences are easy to spot. Black rot usually shows up at the tip of the leaf, the flower sheath, or anywhere that bulb sheaths form a cup to hold water such as around the base of the new growth. Also black rot feels soft, squashy and greasy or wet to the touch. Sunburn usually occurs toward the middle of the leaf in a position exposed directly to the sun—at a bend of the leaf, etc. Sunburn is usually sunken and rough feeling.

The margin between black rot and the clear green tissue is usually yellowish where the infection is spreading. The margin between the sunburn and the clear green tissue is a grayish white and will not continue to spread.

work has just been started on them. This disease is often very hard to recognize as it usually does not kill the plants; if it does, it takes several years to do the job. It is first noticed in the flowers. Earliest signs are a breakdown of the color of the flowers—spotty and blotched coloration of the sepals and petals. In more advanced cases the flowers are crippled and distorted in shape, especially in the petals and lip which become quite twisted and often shorter and heavier than normal. In the later stages it also shows up in the plant. The leaves show a corrugated striping running down them. The tops lengthwise of the ridges are hard and dark green. The valleys between are light yellowish green. In the worst stages the plant growth also becomes distorted. First the leaf tips become indented, and finally the plants put out small twisted and crippled bulbs and leaves.

Control: There is no known treatment for this disease. The safest thing to do is to destroy the whole plant immediately. Burn it! It is not actually known how this disease is transmitted from plant to plant. Most growers feel that sucking insects carry it, and one grower thinks that he spread it through a great many of his plants by using an unsterilized knife when cutting flowers. At any rate, it does not pay to take chances with this disease, and destroying a single plant is cheap insurance against spreading it to your other plants. Professional growers always destroy such plants immediately when they show up, and as this disease is quite rare, the chances are small that the hobby grower will ever see such plants. Don't worry about it, but if such a plant does show up and you are sure of the symptoms, *don't take any chances—destroy it.*

AVOID SPREADING CONTAGIOUS INFECTIONS   Virus, bacteria and fungus infections spread easily and quickly when given a chance. Any infected plant should be isolated from other plants as soon as the infection is noticed. Treatment should be given as recommended above and plant should be kept isolated for at least a week or two until you are sure that the infection is under control.

Most common ways for infections to spread are:

1. *In Water*—Water dripping from an infected plant onto a healthy one—dipping plants in same water or water solution of fertilizer or spray.

2. *On tools*—Knives, scissors, clippers, et cetera, used to divide or trim plants and cut flowers can transfer in-

fections from plant to plant. All tools should be sterilized after every use. This can be done by carefully flaming blades with a match or by immersion for several minutes in 99 per cent alcohol. When cutting out infected areas sterilize between every cut.

3. *In pots*—Old pots can hold and carry infections. All pots should be sterilized by overnight soaking in a strong Chlorox solution before you reuse them.

4. *By insects*—Many infections can be carried from one plant to another by insects which go from one to the other when feeding on the plants. This is another important reason for good insect control.

BE CAREFUL—A little care can save a lot of grief!

chapter 9

A Home of Their Own

INTRODUCTION

There is one other disease not mentioned in the last chapter which is undoubtedly by far the worst of all orchid diseases. It is commonly known as *orchiditis*, and it affects humans, not plants. Once you are infected with orchiditis, you are always and steadily acquiring more plants until either you move the plants out of your home, or you move out yourself. When this situation arises, then your plants need a home of their own.

Before you build a home for your orchids, there are several things that you should consider:

    1. What type will be best for the plants in your climate.

    2. What type fits in best with your home and landscaping.

    3. What type is best for *your* use and enjoyment.

    4. The location from the standpoints of growing conditions for the plants and for your convenience in use and enjoyment.

    5. The cost of the construction—whether to have the job done professionally or whether you can do it yourself. The cost of the materials, and here it is well to consider how long the materials will last. Oftentimes it is better to use somewhat more expensive materials which will more than pay for themselves by outlasting the cheaper substitutes. Also the cost of heat should be carefully considered.

    6. Method of heating must be considered from several standpoints—which type is best for the plants (some types

are much more drying than others), which type is most convenient, and which type is most dependable.

7. It is wise to plan your orchid housing project with an eye toward the future expansion of your collection. Also plan so that you can add on to your building as your collection grows.

IN NORTHERN CLIMATES   *With freezing temperatures*

1. You will need some sort of greenhouse. Keep in mind that the plants want temperatures of from 60° to 80° F. and that they want practically full sun in the winter, about half sun in the summer, that they want humidity from 40 to 70 per cent, and that some provision must be made for ventilation of the house.

2. Whenever possible, plan the greenhouse to fit in with your home and landscaping. Build the foundation and lower walls of the same materials as the house. Build it so that it can be blended into the landscaping. This is not important to the orchids, but you have to live with it, too. A greenhouse can be an awful eyesore. Unfortunately, most greenhouses are, and there is no reason for this as they can actually be designed very attractively. This will cost a little extra, but it is worth it. If you are willing to spend the money, you can have an architect design it, and in the long run, it will be worth it from the standpoint of your satisfaction and enjoyment, to say nothing of your neighbor's feelings in the matter.

3. Traditionally a greenhouse is simply stuck out in the backyard by the garage and is considered part of the service yard. Among other things, this is inconvenient because you have to go outside to reach it, and such a greenhouse will need a separate heating unit. In recent years the trend is to build your greenhouse onto your home. Plan it as an integral part of the living area. There are many attractive, easy and practical ways to do this. You can convert a sunroom, enclose a porch, terrace, or carport to make very suitable growing areas for your plants, or you can build a greenhouse onto the side of the home, opening out from the sunroom, living

room, dining room, breakfast nook or kitchen. In every way possible you should design such a greenhouse to tie into the home. With the same materials, carry out the same or complementary color scheme. Use large, double doors and glass walls opening into the home. In this way you can bring the tropics indoors all winter long. There are many advantages to this. In the first place, it gives you extra living area. Many attractive greenhouses are designed with this in mind, with a central open area, a flagged or brick floor, and informal furniture, such as wrought iron or rattan.

Actually, this need not be as expensive as it sounds. Building onto the home saves a great deal of money in several ways. You use the outside wall of your house for one or possibly two walls of the greenhouse, and usually you can use the same heating system which you already have in your home, merely extending it into the greenhouse. Such a greenhouse also adds to the charm, beauty, and value of your home, and last but not least, it is much more convenient to use since you don't have to go outside. This means that you will enjoy it more. You will spend more time in it, and it will be much easier to show to your guests and friends. Such a greenhouse becomes a part of your everyday living and gives many hours of pleasure.

4. The location for your greenhouse must be chosen carefully as regards exposure to the sun. South is best, east or west will do, and the northern exposure should never even be considered. You also should consider the best location for connecting onto the home—the best place to connect to the heating and the place giving the most convenience, enjoyment, use and beauty to you as part of your home.

5. The cost of your greenhouse is another point to be considered carefully. Greenhouses can be expensive, but they don't have to be. Size and type of greenhouse chosen has a great deal to do with cost. A wood frame house is the cheapest and easiest to build and if finest grades of wood are used, will last as long and well as any other type. The actual building of the house can also be expensive. Having it done by a professional is expensive, but you are sure of getting a good

job. The home craftsman familiar with hammer and saw can build a good greenhouse easily. There are several ready-made kit types of greenhouses on the market which are especially designed for you to put up yourself. The Lord and Burnham Company of Irvington, New York, makes such a kit greenhouse called the Orlyt, which is very satisfactory and inexpensive and can be built by anyone who can use a hammer and a screw driver.

The materials that you use in building your greenhouse will determine expenses to a great extent, but don't skimp on buying the better grades because they cost a little more. The constant humidity and watering in the greenhouse are very hard on poor materials, and the extra expense in the beginning will be small in comparison with the cost of repairs and replacements later on. All wood used in a greenhouse should be treated with a wood preservative before use and should be kept well painted always.

6.   Heating is one of the big expenses in a greenhouse, both to install and to run. As far as the plants are concerned, you can use coal, oil, gas (enclosed flame units) or electricity (in Iceland hot springs are used). Hot-air heat is the poorest type for a greenhouse because it is so drying. Circulating hot-water heat and electricity are the least drying methods of heating a greenhouse. Find out which method is cheapest in your part of the country. By far the cheapest method anywhere is to connect onto your home system. This is cheap to install and will add little extra expense to your fuel bill. The most important thing about the heating system you use is that it should be a steady, dependable supply, requiring the least possible amount of work for the sake of your enjoyment. This is another reason why connecting into the home system is advisable and satisfactory. Your home heating is much more likely to be a steady and sure supply, less likely to break down or go out of kilter than a small, inexpensive unit, and it will add no extra work to your daily chores. If it is possible, you should have an individual thermostat control in your greenhouse, and it is also advisable to have a thermostatic warning device to wake you up in the

middle of the night in case of heat failure or sudden and drastic drops in temperature. Your heating system should also be capable of handling quick temperature drops as greenhouses are very subject to outside changes of temperature. Glass transmits heat and cold readily. The heating system should be capable of keeping your greenhouse at a minimum night temperature of 60° F. The sun will usually push the temperature up during the day.

7. One other point is ofen ignored and always comes up to plague you afterwards. *Build big enough for future expansion of your collection.* You will do well to figure out how big you need your greenhouse now; then build it about twice as big, and while you're at it, don't ignore the possibility of wanting to extend the house even more later on. This may seem extreme, but actually experience shows that it is more likely the bare minimum. Funny as it seems, nobody ever gets less plants. They always seem to multiply, and you will acquire more and then more. Plan for it in the beginning and be prepared. If you plan for expansion of your greenhouse in the beginning, it can be done in an attractive manner. If you don't, it will soon look like the house that Jack built.

INEXPENSIVE PLASTIC GREENHOUSES

Recent advances in the manufacture of plastic in thin sheets and film offer fine possibilities for the "do-it-yourself" orchid grower who wants a greenhouse but can't afford a glass one. There are now several plastics on the market that are suitable for greenhouse use. One of the best (but also most expensive) is Dupont's Weatherable Mylar, Type W. Others that also show promise are Bakelite U-V poly-vinyl-chloride and Bakelite Krene. Many others are now being experimented with and the next few years should come up with many worth-while advances in this field.

A few of the advantages and disadvantages of plastic greenhouses, as well as brief comments on the use of plastics in greenhouse design and construction, are included here. This is a new field, however, and since much of this work is still experimental, few definite instructions and little factual data can be given. He who builds with plastic at this point is definitely a pioneer and will have to learn much from his own trial and error experimentation.

First, it should be pointed out that the plastics now available will not last as long as glass in greenhouse construction. If you can afford a standard glass greenhouse, it will undoubtedly last longer than a plastic one. However, there are other considerations besides lasting quality that may be important to you.

1. Plastics are less expensive than glass to begin with and much less expensive to build with. Plastics are light and tough. This makes building easier and less expensive.

2. Anyone normally proficient with hammer, saw and staple-gun can build a plastic greenhouse. Expensive professional builders are not necessary.

3. Plastics are flexible and easy to work with. This is particularly important regarding the design of your greenhouse. Glass houses are quite limited in design possibilities. Plastic houses are almost unlimited as to design.

Points to consider when planning your plastic greenhouse

Light-shade—Light intensity is lower in winter, higher in summer. Therefore you will need to consider methods of shading that can be used in summer, easily removed in winter. A saran shade cloth over-tent is one of the easiest and best methods. Do not paint plastic greenhouses with white lead or other greenhouse shading compounds. These are hard to get off in winter and may harm plastics by chemical action.

Build onto your home—You can use strong house wall as steady support, to build onto. This makes it easier, less expensive to build.

HOW TO USE PLASTICS IN A GREENHOUSE

Plastics are pliable, flexible, and must be supported to avoid sagging. Stretch until just barely smooth-tight, then staple down with staple gun.

. . . staple every 2 to 4 inches, at least ½ inch in from edge.

. . . cover stapled edges with molding or lath, nailing strip; nail every 6 to 8 inches.

. . . use a nailing strip ½ to 1 inch wider than rafter underneath. This shades plastic adjacent to rafter and will make it last considerably longer.

. . . rafters or frame work should support plastic at close intervals—18 to 27 inches apart.

Most plastics are elastic.

. . . will stretch under rain water or snow load.

. . . therefore your roof must have a good pitch so that runoff is fast.

. . . minimum 1 foot drop in 2 feet of width.

Plastics come on a roll, and most are from 36 to 54 inches wide.

. . . we recommend spacing supporting rafters at ½ this width, approximately 18 to 27 inches apart. We measure from outside of first frame to far side of third frame for full width of plastic *so that we have a full overlap* where plastic joins.

. . . overlaps are covered tightly with lath or molding, nailed down every 6 to 8 inches. This gives very tight house, much more air-tight than a glass house.

Apply plastic in strips running across

. . . on lean-to type house, start at top, run down rafters, over eaves and down side posts to ground.

. . . on free standing house stretch plastic from ground on one side up across top and down to ground on other side.

. . . should be drawn taut and stapled carefully to insure an even, unwrinkled and unstrained cover. *Stretch the plastic just barely smooth—not tight enough to put a strain on it.*

. . . cementing or heat sealing of seams is not necessary or advisable.

Double glazing of the house is advisable

. . . simply cover house with a second layer of plastic on inside of rafters and frames.

. . . this gives best insulation, like a storm window.

. . . makes house much more air tight.

. . . easier to heat in winter.

. . . easier to keep cool in summer.

. . . much less subject to quick changes in outside temperature.

. . . a 2 inch space between outside and inside covering is best. This gives best insulation, wider space allows convection currents to form.

. . . for this reason, we recommend using 2-inch lumber for rafters and frames.

. . . inside glazing can be very thin, even 1 mil. thickness will
do.

. . . double glazing makes humidity easier to maintain.

. . . stops condensation and drip from roof.

. . . makes heating much cheaper—up to 50 per cent.

. . . gives double protection against puncture.

Plastics are tough and durable

. . . resistant to pressure and hard shocks.

. . . don't break like glass.

  Most subject to

. . . puncture from sharp objects.

. . . deterioration from sun.

  Sun is worst enemy

. . . in summer when sun is most intense, should be partially
shaded.

. . . cut out half of sunlight.

. . . plastics will last twice as long.

Best protection for plastic

. . . shading plastic house with saran shade screen.

. . . saran made into tent over house.

. . . about 2 feet above plastic.

In far South

. . . shade tent can stay up year round.

In North

. . . shade tent should be taken down and stored from early fall
till late spring. Use only for intense summer sun. Saran
folds easily like a tarpaulin for storage.

. . . several companies will supply saran cut and sewn to order
with grommets for easy put-up and take-down.

Breakdown of plastic shows up as

  1. Brittleness (loss of flexibility—stretchability).
  2. Discoloration or change of color.

. . . This can be dangerous if it occurs during cold winter
weather.

IMPORTANT

  1. Check closely and often for signs of breakdown or
puncture.

2. Make a thorough check of whole greenhouse *every* year in late summer or fall and replace all plastic that shows any sign of breakdown or wear.

3. Keep an extra supply of plastic on hand at all times for emergency repair. If kept dry and in the dark, it will last well.

All wood used in greenhouse building should be

either: Heart Cypress or Redwood (both of which are expensive).

or: Inexpensive woods can be used if pressure-treated with a good wood preservative.

Creosoted wood is all right if well dried and cured. Freshly creosoted wood should not be used near live plants. Wood pressure-treated with copper salts lasts just about as well and this can be stained for a more attractive finish.

We recommend two coats of Cuprinol or Cop-r-tox (with wood stain added to match your color scheme) in addition to the pressure treatment. This seals the wood surface and makes it last better as well as making an attractive finish. It has been our experience that painted wood does not last as long as wood-treated as recommended above.

The wood frame of your greenhouse, if properly treated, will last for many years, through many replacements of the plastic covering. Plastic will need replacing at least every 2 to 5 years. Frame should last a lifetime. Plastic is quick, easy and inexpensive to replace. Use of double-head galvanized nails on plastic nailing strips makes them easy to pull and replace when replacing plastic.

Foundation for greenhouse

. . . should be solid and permanent.

. . . match home—block, brick, stone.

. . . best to go below frostline.

3 feet in Chicago area

more in colder areas

less in warmer areas.

If you don't want to build a permanent foundation, only upright wooden corner posts and main posts along sides need be buried below frost line. The plastic should go all the way down

to ground and loose earth should be piled up against foot of
plastic wall to make a tight seal.

. . . wood underground will rot faster than rest of frame work,
should be well treated. Creosote is best for wood used
under ground.

Additional Information on Plastic Greenhouse

Contact your local County Agricultural Agent. He will be able to
tell you of any in your locality. The Agriculture Department of your
State College or University can probably help considerably on this
subject as well. Several information sheets and greenhouse patterns
are now available, as listed below:

"Low Cost Plastic Greenhouses" by E. M. Emmert, Agri. Experiment Station, Univ. of Kentucky, Lexington, Kentucky.

"Cornell Plastic Panel Greenhouse" by Raymond Sheldrake,
Dept. of Vegetable Crops, Cornell University, Ithaca, New
York.

"Do-it-Yourself Plastic Greenhouses"—Fennell Orchid Company, Homestead, Florida.

Build it Yourself Greenhouse Pattern No. 571—Easi-bild Pattern Co., Pleasantville, New York.

IN THE TROPICS AND SUB-TROPICS   *Where there is no serious*
danger of heavy frosts or freezes, a greenhouse is not necessary or
even desirable. The best type of house for orchids in such a climate
is one which gives them the outdoor growing conditions which they
like but does supply some control of sun and perhaps water.

1. As we know, most of the plants need about one-half
shade the year round in such climates. They may also need
some wind protection and some rain protection during certain seasons of the year. A simple lath house supplies the
first two requirements. The simplest kind of lath house is
merely a square or rectangular box or lean-to built of alternate
laths and spaces between. This is a functional and practical
type of house for your orchids. A lath house with a glass top
supplies all three requirements, and everything considered,
is by far the best type of house for year-round growing. In
the tropics and sub-tropics such a house with a slightly sloped
shed roof of glass is easy to build and actually is much better

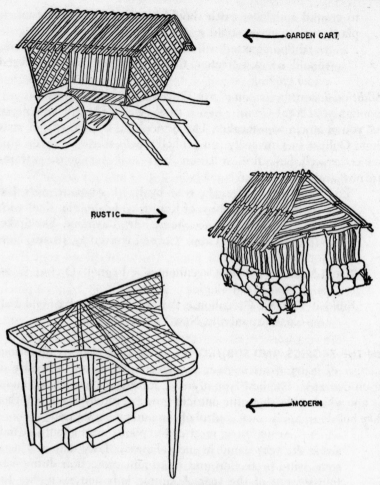

GARDEN CART

RUSTIC

MODERN

22. LATH HOUSES.

for the plants than a greenhouse. During the hot summer months a greenhouse in the tropics gets much too hot and muggy and requires too much shade and spraying to keep down temperatures. This results in soft, weak growths which do not flower well. Growing conditions in a lath house actually amount to outdoor conditions with controls. Under such outdoor conditions, which are so much closer to the natural conditions that orchids like, plants grow much stronger and harder, have more resistance to insects, disease and abuse, and flower more heavily with flowers of heavier substance, which last longer.

2. The most wonderful thing about a lath house is that it is flexible in design, can be built to match any surroundings of house or garden: rustic, traditional, ranch-style, modern or functional. A lath house can be designed as a garden cart (Fig. 22), bird cage, summerhouse, a rustic hut, or an arbor. This is another great advantage over greenhouses. You can use any material to fit into any design.

3. Lath houses should be planned for beauty and effective display of plants as well as for growing. Consider your own comfort and the accessibility of the house as well as the requirements of the plants. The trend is to design your lath house as a part of your home. Use it to extend your living area. Screen it in so that it doubles as a sun porch, terrace, or patio, as well as for growing your plants. Add it onto a porch, lanai or a Florida room; or build it onto the living room, dining room, kitchen or breakfast nook. Such a lath house can supply a very interesting view and act as a screen between you and your neighbors. It can be designed to bring your plant hobby indoors as a part of your decorating scheme and everyday living. Naturally this will make your hobby more thoroughly enjoyable, both to your family and to your guests. A lath house with a glass top supplies an outdoor living area which is usable in all weather. Many people now have their architects design the lath house right into the home. This is a good idea to insure the most attractive job.

4. Location is important, and there are several points to consider. Your lath house should have an unshaded exposure to the sun for at least half a day, and if possible, it should be sheltered from cold, northwest winds and any constant drying winds which you may have in your location. The southern exposure is best as it allows ample sun. Your house, walls, garage or shrubbery and trees to the north will cut out north winds. East or west would also be all right, but northern exposures are not good unless they are far enough

from the house or other shade to allow ample sun exposure. If you have prevailing winds from one direction, it is best to locate your lath house in the lee of some shelter or build the lath house walls solid on the side toward the winds. Avoid solid walls all the way around a lath house. This defeats the purpose of a lath house as conditions inside will be much too stuffy. If you feel that your plants need shelter from wind on all sides, build the walls solid only on the middle section of the wall. Start your solid wall halfway from the floor to the bench and end it a foot or two below the roof. This shelters the plants themselves from the wind while allowing good ventilation below and above.

5. The cost of building a lath house is usually quite low. Most of the work you should be able to do yourself. Unless you are planning a very fancy one, it should require little heavy or skilled construction work. You can use almost any material in building a slat house. The growing conditions supplied are most important. The cost of materials and their lasting qualities are next most important. The materials used should supply about 50 per cent shade in alternate stripes or spots of sun and shade, and such spots or stripes should not be much more than 2 inches wide.

Natural rock or masonry walls and posts are, of course, almost indestructible and can supply a very rustic effect.

Tree trunks, limbs and branches are also quite attractive and rustic but will not last very long.

Wood is easy to work with, especially for the home carpenter, but will not last long unless heavily treated with a good wood preservative, such as Cuprinol, and all wood should be kept above ground at all times. *Don't bury wooden posts in the ground.* Use concrete or pipe footings and attach the wood to them above ground level.

Metal strips like those used in Venetian blinds can take the place of wooden laths and are said to be very satisfactory. They can be used quite effectively for a modernistic effect.

Plastic screen shading is now on the market and seems to be very satisfactory for orchid plants. It comes in various weights, giving different amounts of shade and should be used in a weight which gives only a little more than 50 per cent shade. Plants grow very well under this screen, and it is especially satisfactory in that it can double as an insect screen as well.

Galvanized pipe framework for your house is very practical as it lasts almost forever with little or no upkeep (a lath house built with pipe framework and a plastic screen top and sides should last indefinitely with almost no upkeep and supplies wonderful growing conditions for the plants).

Fiber-glass sheeting is new and unproven as yet. No one knows how long it will last, and it is expensive. It has several great advantages, however. It is flexible and easy to work with. It can be sawed and nailed. WARNING: Avoid green fiber glass as it cuts out the part of the spectrum of light which plants need.

One serious disadvantage that has developed with fiber glass, here in Florida at least, is that after the surface has weathered a little bit, fungus gets in and grows down through the plastic matrix along the glass fibers. This makes the fiber glass look dirty and gradually darkens the whole house. Less light comes through for the plants. This is a serious problem here but it may not be in northern climates.

In the long run it pays to use good materials. The conditions of sun, water and humidity are hard on almost all building materials. Build to last; repairs and replacements are expensive.

6.   Heating luckily is not necessary in a lath house. Lath-house-grown plants are hardy and can stand a great deal of variation in temperature. If your lath house will be subject to sweeping cold winds, curtains or shutters for the north and west sides may be advisable. The shade roof or glass top will keep frost from settling on the plants.

7.   Build your slat house big enough for the expansion of your collection. Figure out your present needs, then build considerably larger. You will need it sooner than you believe. Plan with an eye to future additions. This will insure a better-looking final product. You may not think you'll ever enlarge it, but you will.

chapter 10

Orchids Under Artificial Light

Insufficient light is probably the most common single problem facing the indoor gardener. Modern homes seem very well lighted and many people fail to realize that plants need a great deal more light to grow properly than is usually present for our comfort when reading. Plants can easily starve to death for lack of sufficient light in a location perfectly well lighted for our normal needs of reading or working.

Light is normally measured in foot-candles. The average home is usually lighted to an intensity of 40 to 60 foot-candles. Plants in the garden often receive up to 10,000 foot-candles and greenhouse plants, depending on type and their requirements, receive from 500 to 2,500 or 3,000 foot-candles of light.

Insufficient light in moderate degree is often the cause of poor bloom or lack of bloom on otherwise healthy appearing plants. A serious lack of light causes plants to grow tall and spindly with weak, dark-colored growth that never flowers and often cannot even support itself, but must be tied up.

Artificial Light as a supplement to natural lighting is of considerable advantage for parts of the country with much dark winter weather, or in cases where the window is partially shaded or obscured by trees or adjoining buildings. Lights can be mounted over the plant shelves in the window or on either side of the window behind the curtains or draperies. Fluorescent lights are best for this purpose and care must be used to keep them close to the plants for best results (details of distance from lights to plants are discussed below). These lights should be used only during daylight hours for the reasons explained further on, as the use of them at night may well prohibit blooming.

The use of artificial light entirely instead of sun is also practical for plant growth when proper sunlight is not available. With careful planning and the proper setup, it is possible to convert any spare room in your home; garage, service room, basement or attic to a plant room. Such a room will give you a great deal of pleasure and in some ways, at least, you will find it easier and less expensive than a greenhouse.

Two factors about light are important when planning a setup for growing plants under artificial light: The *intensity* of light necessary for proper growth and flowering and the *quality* of the light to be used.

Light intensity is very important as different plants require different intensities for proper growth. African Violets, Episcias, Philodendron and most foliage plants will do well under relatively low light intenseness; from 400 to 500 foot-candles. Most orchids and many other flowering plants require considerably higher light intensities. Normal lighting in the average home runs only about 40 foot-candles so it is obvious that even for plants of low intensity requirements special lighting will have to be set up. Below is a list of recommended intensities necessary for some types of orchids:

Seedlings in flasks: Start at 400-500 foot-candles,
increase with growth to 600-700 foot candles.

Community Pots and small individual pot seedlings	700-800 ″	″
Cypripediums, Phalaenopsis and other shade lovers	600-800 ″	″
Mature Cattleyas, Most Oncidiums and some Epidendrums and Dendrobiums	1000-1200 ″	″
Most strap-leaved Vandas, Cymbidiums and many Dendrobiums and other sun lovers	1200-1500 ″	″

A light meter will prove of great help on checking these intensities. Your camera store should be able to help with this and tell you how to convert meter readings to foot candles. The customer service department of your local power or light company can also help with this and will probably take foot-candle readings for you and advise on proper setups from the wiring standpoint.

Quality of light used is equally important. Regular incandescent or Tungsten filament lights give off a great deal of heat and if used close enough to the plants and in sufficient quantity to supply the necessary intensity, they will burn the foliage. Also these bulbs give only part of the necessary light spectrum for proper growth; they supply enough of the red part of the spectrum but not enough of the blue.

Fluorescent or mercury vapor lamps do not put out as much heat and can be used almost touching the foliage without burning, so that proper light intensity is possible. These tube lights give plenty of the blue spectrum but not enough of the red. The new deluxe cool white tubes give a better balance of the spectrum for plant growth than do the common Daylight or "blue" types, but even these do not give sufficient red for best plant growth and flowering.

Therefore, to give the plants the necessary balance of blue and red light qualities, *a combination of incandescent and fluorescent light is necessary.* Recommendations for the best balance varies with the different workers in the field. Some recommend one 40 W. incandescent bulb to every 40 W. fluorescent fixture; another recommends 2 25 W. incandescent bulbs spaced out and strung alongside each 40 W. fluorescent fixture. Still another researcher recommends 10 per cent of the foot-candle intensity from incandescent lights and 90 per cent from fluorescent tubes. In all, they agree on deriving most of the intensity from the cool fluorescent light and using as little as possible of the hot incandescent lights—only enough to supply the necessary red part of the spectrum.

Many types of suitable light fixtures are readily available from your local lamp and lighting stores. The most important single factor is to have really good reflectors for all of your lights so that the maximum intensity can be directed straight onto the plants. Regular commercial reflectors are fine for this. Two typical units of the common 40 W. 2-tube types mounted side by side with 2 40 W. incandescent lights mounted between them and spaced out about ¼ way in from each end of the flourescent fixtures will light a 4 x 4 foot table quite evenly. These lights, suspended 1 foot above the leaf tips, will give an average light intensity of 500-600 foot-candles.

For higher intensities, single tube fluorescent fixtures can be mounted on a plywood backing in parallel rows. Spaced 4 inches apart, center to center, on a surface of high reflectance such as an aluminum foil covered surface or a glossy-white enamel painted surface, these tubes will deliver an intensity of 1000 to 1200 foot-candles, at a distance of 1 foot from the tubes. The addition of the necessary number of incandescent bulbs (1 40 W. bulb or 2 25 W. bulbs to each 2 of the standard fluorescent tubes) will boost this intensity close to the 1500 foot-candle level.

The light intensity from any light source varies inversely with the square of the distance from the light to the subject. In other words, when you move the light twice as far away from the plants you have only ¼ the intensity on the plants; three times as far away and you have only ⅑ as much light on the plants. If you move the light closer, it increases in the same amount. Cut the distance in half and you have 4 times the amount of light intensity. This is extremely important as it means you cannot mount the lights on the ceiling and grow your plants on a table of normal height. *The lights must be mounted directly above the plants and probably not more than 12 inches above the leaf tips.* For the same reason, plants out to the sides of the lights will not get as much light intensity as those directly under the lights. Also, fluorescent tubes give the most intensity toward the center of their length. Therefore, if you are growing plants of varying light intensity requirements, you should group the plants wanting the most intensity in the center of the tables and then work out toward the edges with those of increasingly lower light intensity requirements. By careful placing of the individual plants, one can grow those with varying requirements all under the same lights. Individual plants can be given more or less light by raising or lowering them as well. Set them up on inverted pots or supply a higher shelf for those requiring the most light. Those requiring less light should be lower down.

For the practical purposes of watering and other handling of the plants, a space of about 12 inches from lights to plants is just about the minimum. Some growers prefer to mount the bulbs on a movable mounting hanging from the ceiling on pulleys. In this manner, the lights can be raised out of the way for watering and working on the plants, and then lowered back down to almost touching for highest intensities. Also one end or side can be adjusted higher or lower to give varying intensities or to match different plant heights. The flexibility of such a set-up has many advantages.

Other growers have built two- or three-decker setups which are not movable but in such cases the spaces between shelves usually vary to allow for different heights of plants and to supply varying intensities for a wider range of growing conditions. If floor space is a problem, then these two- and three-level setups have definite advantages too, as they allow for many more plants in a restricted area.

Hours of light—The number of hours these lights are used each day is also of utmost importance as plants require both darkness and light for proper growth. Part of the natural functions of all plants take place during daylight; another part of these natural functions require darkness in order to carry through normally. Thus all plants require alternating periods of darkness and light.

Best plant growth seems to be produced with a sixteen-hour day and an eight-hour night. For seedlings, back bulbs, cuttings and other forms of purely vegetative growth, a steady sixteen-hour day is recommended.

However, the blooming season of many plants is regulated by the seasonal changes in day length. Thus some plants bloom when the days get shorter, others when the days get longer. Therefore, *a steady length of day*, such as the sixteen-hour recommendation for vegetative growth *will cause some plants to bloom out of season and will prohibit many plants from blooming at all*. This response of the blooming of some plants according to the length of day is called the Photo-periodic response and is a very involved subject. By careful shading at some times of the year or by adding extra hours of light at other times, it is possible to control the blooming date of many orchids and other flowers. The Cornell University Agricultural Experiment Station at Ithaca, New York, has done a great deal of work on this subject and has published some of these findings in their Bulletins. Since this is an involved technique, it is better suited for commercial growers than it is for the home grower.

The safest and most practical way to handle this problem is to *give your plants under artificial light the same hours of light as they would have out of doors*. Give them a normal seasonal change of day length by turning on the lights at dawn and turning them off at night fall. An automatic time-clock will be a big help on this project. It can be set to turn the lights off and on automatically at whatever hours you choose, and these settings can be changed every one or two weeks to correspond with the seasonal changes in day length outdoors. By this method, your plants will bloom at their normal season and you will be able to depend upon them just as if they were growing under natural light.

A *time-clock is almost necessary for any artificial light setup as regularity is of utmost importance*. Just a few hours too many or too few of light once or twice a week can throw off proper blooming seasons or prohibit blooming all together. Few of us have regular enough habits to enjoy a time schedule as exact as the plants will require and an automatic time-clock is relatively inexpensive and so easy to use that it is not only a wonderful convenience, but really a necessity. Just remember that the automatic settings must be changed every one or two weeks to give the necessary normal seasonal change in day length and the time-clock will do the rest of the work for you automatically.

Growing Hints Under Artificial Light—The use of artificial light is no cure-all for general house plant troubles. It will not overcome poor culture or negligence. Good growing conditions in all other phases and careful supervision are just as necessary under artificial lights as anywhere else, but it will help greatly where lack of light is the limiting factor, and you can expect some startling results.

Ventilation is important for all plants and is often ignored in indoor plant rooms. One or two small fans to keep the air stirred up around your plants will prove beneficial. For a small area, a small oscillating fan is ideal. For larger areas or plant rooms, two small fans in opposite corners and pointing towards each other in parallel directions will give good circulation. This ventilation does away with much of the leaf-fungus problems and makes for stronger, healthier growth in general.

If your lighted area is small and confined, the lights may give off enough heat to be a problem. In this case, a small exhaust fan hooked up to an inexpensive thermostat will help.

Temperature—The higher the temperature, the more light is required for proper growth. Therefore, there is no advantage to growing the plants any warmer than necessary. Most orchids and other house plants will do well at daytime temperatures of 65-70° F. At night, most can stand it down to 55 or 60° F. Seedlings will grow better and cuttings and back bulbs will root better at higher temperatures—70° F. to 80° F.

Humidity in the heated home is also a problem, yet it is necessary for good growth. In a plant room, benches or shelves can be built containing a tray-top filled with damp gravel on which the plants sit. This is also a convenience when watering, as it catches overflow and drip too. Some growers have large flat tin pans made for the floor and the benches sit in these. Plastic sheeting can also be used for a floor covering to catch drip and hold water for evaporation and humidity.

Plastic curtains can be used to close in a plant corner in a larger room and confine the humidity to this smaller area.

Black plastic is also available to fence in the light if it should prove objectionable in the rest of the room.

Additional Heat in basement, attic or other poorly heated rooms can be supplied easily by installing thermostatically controlled soil heating cables in the gravel humidity pans. These are available from your garden supply store. Also inexpensive are chick-brooder thermostats which can be connected to incandescent bulbs or small, electric, space heaters under the benches for small additional heating requirements.

Plants can be removed from the lighted area periodically for display in and around the home but should be returned to the growing area soon for rejuvenation and proper maintenance.

chapter 11

Growing Orchids from Seed

Growing orchids from seed is a highly developed science in itself and requires a good laboratory technique. It is not something to be attempted lightly, but it is quite a challenge to most orchid growers. Actually, it is lots of fun to try. When you have grown your own orchids from seed, it is indeed an achievement to be proud of. Few amateurs do much growing from seed, but many do want to try it just to say that they have done so.

In the early days of orchid culture, it was almost impossible to grow orchids from seed, and the grower who managed to grow even two or three plants from a seed pod considered himself lucky. In the early 1900's, scientists in France and Germany found out that a certain fungus sometimes helped orchid seeds to germinate, and they worked out a very involved and complicated method of growing orchids in bottles inoculated with this special fungus. The method was a good one, except that it was so hard to make sure that you had the right fungus for the job, and only that one special fungus. If any other fungus was also present, the system would not work. In the 1920's, Dr. Lewis Knudson at Cornell found out that the fungus was helping the orchid plants by converting starch to sugar and further discovered that by adding sugar to the jelly on which the plants were grown in the bottles, there was no more need for the fungus. As the fungus was so hard to control, the Knudson method was much safer and became very popular. By the Knudson method it is now possible to raise almost every seed from a seed pod. This discovery is undoubtedly one of the most important steps in the history of orchid culture. It changed the whole setup of the orchid business, and it changed orchid growing from a hobby of the very rich to the hobby of housewives and backyard gardeners.

Many growers now make a business of growing orchids from seed. These specialists have greatly increased the variety and quality of orchid flowers through hybridization, introducing many new and finer types. Through cross-breeding and hybridization, we now have orchids almost every size, color and shape imaginable, and we have been able to increase greatly the strength of the plants, ease of culture, and the number of flowers produced. Through careful breeding it has also been possible to produce orchids of almost every type for blooming any time the year round. From this you can see that there are many things to be considered when making a hybrid cross.

Only the finest parent plants should be used. They should possess fine qualities in all of the above categories, and it is also important that they should have the ability to pass on these fine qualities to their progeny. (There is no way to be sure of this unless the previous breeding history of a particular plant is known. Hence the importance of using known parent plants in breeding.) Once upon a time an orchid was simply an orchid, but today the quality of orchid flowers has been improved so highly that it is no longer enough simply to raise more orchids. We have plenty of average quality orchids now, and it is necessary to strive for a consistently higher quality. It doesn't cost any more, and it is no harder to raise the best than it is to produce more of the same old thing. Therefore, if you want to try to raise some orchids from seed, even if it is only for your own fun, you should use seed from the best possible parents. Your final results will be fine. You will have something to show for the work that you have put into them—something to be proud of.

Several growers with very fine stud plants at their disposal now sell orchid seed. The Fennell Orchid Company of Homestead, Florida, was the first orchid company in the world to make a business of selling orchid seed, and they still are the biggest in the seed business today. They sell small quantities of orchid seed, enough for three or four bottles of seedlings, for $5.00. This cost is negligible compared to the amount of effort and time you will put into growing these seeds to mature plants. Of course you can produce your own seed if you want to, and some people prefer to do so for their own personal satisfaction, but the hobby grower seldom has parent plants of equal quality, and the results will not be of

A fine flower of Lc. Wilmosa — a modern hybrid of highest show quality.

A lovely Wedding Bouquet entirely of white orchids, featuring large white *Brassos*, surrounded by *Calanthes, Phalaenopsis* and *Brassavola nodosa*.

Exotic arrangements featuring Vandas and tropical foliage for dramatic effect.

Lc. Autumn Yellow — one of the finest yellows in the orchid world today.

equal quality either. Why fool around with inferior quality when seed from the finest plants is available to you?

If you really want to grow your own, however, the process is simple.

1. *Select your parent plants;* they should be of the *finest possible quality.* Consider all the points listed above. The plant which will carry the seed pod *should be strong,* as the pod stays on close to one year and is quite a drain on the strength of the plant. All commonly grown orchids are both male and female in the same flower, and you can use either plant for either sex. The plant which carries the seed pod is called the female. The plant which supplies the pollen is called the male for that particular crossing. *Flowers used should be fresh.* It is best to pollinate within the first week that the flowers are open. The first three days is wisest. Pollen should come from a fresh flower, too, and should be removed from the flower before it has been open, at the most, two weeks. Fresh pollen is easy to tell by its bright yellow color. If the pollen shows a brownish tinge or any signs of mold or mildew, it should not be used as it is no good. Both parent plants should be from the same general branch of the orchid family. For instance, Cattleyas will cross with Cattleyas, Laelias and Brassavolas, but not with Phalaenopsis, Vandas or Dendrobiums, et cetera.

2. *Remove pollen from the flower.* The pollen is in the form of pellets, not dust, and these pellets are called pollinia. Different types of orchids have a different number of pollinia, varying from two to eight per flower. *The pollinia are located in a small caplike container called the pollen cap, which is at the front end of the sexual column of the flower. This column is usually located either within the tube of the lip or directly above the lip of the flower.* The pollen cap is hinged at the top and can be removed easily with any pointed instrument, such as a pencil, toothpick or knife blade. Reach into the lip of the flower with the pointed instrument under the column. Press the instrument up lightly and slowly draw it out, pressing against the underside of the column. The pollen cap will swing outward from the column on the hinge

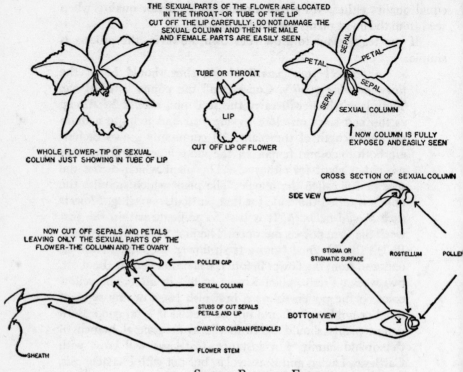

THE SEXUAL PARTS OF THE FLOWER ARE LOCATED
IN THE THROAT-OR TUBE OF THE LIP
CUT OFF THE LIP CAREFULLY ; DO NOT DAMAGE THE
SEXUAL COLUMN AND THEN THE MALE
AND FEMALE PARTS ARE EASILY SEEN

TUBE OR THROAT

LIP

CUT OFF LIP OF FLOWER

WHOLE FLOWER- TIP OF SEXUAL
COLUMN JUST SHOWING IN TUBE OF LIP

PETAL
SEPAL
SEPAL
PETAL
SEPAL
SEPAL

SEXUAL COLUMN

NOW COLUMN IS FULLY
EXPOSED AND EASILY SEEN

NOW CUT OFF SEPALS AND PETALS
LEAVING ONLY THE SEXUAL PARTS OF THE
FLOWER-THE COLUMN AND THE OVARY

POLLEN CAP

SEXUAL COLUMN

STUBS OF CUT SEPALS
PETALS AND LIP

OVARY (OR OVARIAN PEDUNCLE)

FLOWER STEM

SHEATH

CROSS SECTION OF SEXUAL COLUMN

SIDE VIEW

STIGMA OR
STIGMATIC SURFACE   ROSTELLUM   POLLEN

BOTTOM VIEW

23.   SEXUAL PARTS OF FLOWER.

at its top. The sticky bases of the pollinia will attach to the
point of the instrument, and they usually stick tightly to it.
If the pollen is old, it may not be sticky. In this case it helps
to wet the tip of the instrument so that the pollinia will
stick to it. It is best to hold your left hand under the lip of
the flower as you remove the pollinia with your right hand
in order to catch any of the pollen which may not stick to
the instrument. Usually the pollen cap breaks off from the
column and comes out on the instrument with the pollinia
still in it. When this happens, gently pull off the pollen cap;
the pollen will probably stay stuck to the instrument.

3.   You are now ready to pollinate the female flower.
It is wise to *remove the pollen from the female flower before*

you start to insert the pollen from the male flower. This is
to make sure that you do not mix the pollen from the two
flowers, which can happen quite easily. It is also best to *cut
off the sepals, petals and lip of the flower which you are going
to pollinate.* (Fig. 23) This makes it much easier to place
the pollen correctly, and it avoids fungus infection and the
abortion of the seed pod when the flower wilts and folds up
around the column after pollination. Cut carefully and gently
without bruising the flower stem or column. *The female
organ is on the underside of the column at the front. It is
a deep depression just behind the pollen cap.* This depression
is separated from the pollen cap by a dam called the rostellum. The female organ is called the stigma or the stigmatic
surface. It is filled with a sticky gluelike clear liquid. This
is to hold the pollen in the female organ.

4. *Pollinate the flower* by putting the pollen into the
depression with the pointed instrument. Spread out the
pollen evenly in the depression using the tip of the instrument. (Fig. 24) Avoid overlapping or piling up as much as

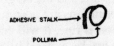

POLLEN CAP, CONTAINS 4 GRAINS
OF POLLINIA EACH ON
AN ADHESIVE STALK

ADHESIVE STALK

POLLINIA

TO POLLINATE A FLOWER THE POLLINIA
SHOULD BE REMOVED FROM THE CAP
AND PLACED IN THE STIGMA

SEXUAL COLUMN

STIGMA

POLLINIA

24. POLLINATING.

possible. It is best to keep the pollen toward the back of
the depression if there is more room than the pollen needs.
*Use all of the pollen from one flower to pollinate the other
flower.* If the flower producing the pollen is much smaller
than the female flower, use the pollen from several flowers
on the one female flower.

5. *Attach a label to the stem of the flower with the
names of the parents and the date* that the cross was made.
The name of the female should be at the top and the name

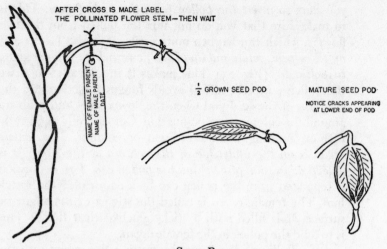

AFTER CROSS IS MADE LABEL
THE POLLINATED FLOWER STEM—THEN WAIT

NAME OF FEMALE PARENT
NAME OF MALE PARENT
DATE

½ GROWN SEED POD

MATURE SEED POD

NOTICE CRACKS APPEARING
AT LOWER END OF POD

25. Seed Pods.

of the male parent should be second. Tie the label at the base of the flower stem. If it is tied along the center of the stem, which is actually the ovary of the flower, it will pinch the seed pod as it expands and cause it to abort.

6. *Now wait.* Most types of orchids take from nine to twelve months for a seed pod to mature, and the pods are seldom good before six months. The plant should be given normal growing care and no special precautions are necessary.

7. *Harvest the pod.* When the pod is ripe, it will crack open and dump out the seed. The cracks appear in the grooves along the sides of the pod, and they start to open at the bottom or column end. First you will notice that the pod will start to turn slightly yellowish along the side grooves and then, soon after, begin to open. Some types open very quickly and dump out the seeds immediately. It takes careful and constant observation to harvest the pod before the seed is lost. When the pod has been cut from the plant, place it on a piece of slick or hard-finish paper, open it fully along the cracks, *and scrape out the seed. Separate the seed from the fuzzy, hairlike chaff;* shake the fuzz gently, and the seed will drop out onto the paper. Orchid seed is the smallest

of all plant seed, almost as fine as face powder. A large pod will contain from one-half to two million seed. Now *fold up the seed in the paper*, and *label the packet as to the parentage and the age* of the seed. *Store the seed in the icebox until ready to use.* DO NOT FREEZE IT. You can keep seed several months or occasionally even several years in the icebox, but its strength and ability to germinate usually weaken with age, and *it is best to use your seed as soon as possible after harvesting*.

8. *Test seed for viability* (the ability to germinate). The surest way to test seed is under a microscope or strong magnifying glass. Seeds look like crudely woven baskets. They are long and narrow, and the husk looks like basket weaving. The live seed has a fat and swollen embryo in the middle of the long, narrow basket. This embryo may have tinges of red, yellow or brown. Actually, the color of the seed as you look at it with the naked eye is a pretty good indication of the good seed present. Bad seed without live embryos is usually white. Good seed is usually darker in color, varying from a cream color to yellowish brown and occasionally dark rusty-red. The darker the seed, the better it is. This color also varies with the type of orchid. Cattleya seed ranges from cream to brownish yellow. It is well to test the seed in order to know whether or not it is worth-while to go to the trouble of planting it. It also helps give you an idea of how heavily the seed should be planted in the bottles. Lighter colored seed should be planted much more heavily than the darker ones as the percentage of live seeds is smaller. Because of the many thousands of seed in a pod, seed with even 1 or 2 per cent embryos is worth planting.

SEED-PLANTING TECHNIQUE   Your results in seed planting will depend upon how closely you follow directions. You must be very painstaking at all times. Every step is necessary, and one slip will cancel out all of your work. Your enemy in seed planting is fungus or bacterial infection. The whole purpose of the planting technique is to get the seed into the sterile bottles without allowing any fungus in, as the fungus will grow much faster than the young orchids and will quickly smother and kill them off. The whole technique is designed to insure a clean planting.

PREPARATION—MATERIALS AND EQUIPMENT NEEDED:

1. *Agar-Agar orchid jelly.* We recommend Knudson's Formula B, which is an Agar-Agar jelly with a complete plant food and sugar. This can be bought ready mixed, or you can make your own. The ready-mix is by far the easiest. All that you have to do is add water and cook it. You should use distilled water because the ready-mix has been adjusted to the correct acidity when distilled water is used. This ready-mix is called Difco Bacto Orchid Agar, and it can be purchased from the Difco Laboratories, Detroit 1, Michigan. They sell it in ¼ lb. and 1 lb. packages. The ¼ lb. package is enough for several bottles. If you are planning to plant only a few bottles, the ready-mix is definitely preferable because, should you mix your own, the smallest quantity you can buy of each of the several ingredients would, in many cases, be enough for one hundred or more bottles. Some people, however, do prefer to mix their own as they feel that they have a fresh mix each time they use it, and they can adjust the pH at the time of mix. (pH is the measure of acidity or alkalinity in the jelly, and it must be adjusted very carefully or the formula will not jell.)

KNUDSON'S FORMULA B

Calcium Nitrate	1.00 gram
Monobasic Potassium Phosphate	0.25 gram
Magnesium Sulfate	0.25 gram
Ammonium Sulfate	0.50 gram
Sucrose (white sugar)	20.00 grams
Ferrous Sulfate	0.025 gram
Agar (Difco Bacto Agar)	15-17.5 grams
Distilled water	1. liter (1000 cc)

2. *Phosphoric Acid* for adjusting pH if you mix your own. Only a small quantity is needed.

3. *Non-absorbent and absorbent cotton*—A small quantity of each.

4. *Mercurochrome*

5. *Bottles for planting the seed*—Most people use 500 cc Ehrlemeyer flasks. We prefer to use 32-ounce prescription bottles. They have a flat side so that they lie well without rolling, and they have more flat area for planting the seed.

6. *Single-hole rubber stoppers* to fit tightly in the neck of the flasks or bottles.

7. *Small square pieces of cloth* about six inches on the side, one per bottle.

8. *String* to tie cloth around bottle necks.

9. *Calcium hypochlorite* (70% chlorine—obtainable from chemical supply or dairy supply houses).

10. *S.T. 37* (trade name) from drugstore.

11. *A detergent* such as Joy, or other wetting agent to break surface tension.

12. *A funnel* with *filter paper* or Kleenex.

13. *Several small bottles*, 2- to 3-ounce, preferably with *glass stoppers*.

14. *Medicine dropper*.

15. *Glass dish* large enough and deep enough to wash your hands in.

16. *Household spray gun*, such as a Flit gun (cheapest one possible because the disinfecting solution will ruin it quickly).

17. *Pressure cooker* large enough to hold your bottles.

18. *Rubber gloves*—long-sleeved type; should reach almost to elbow.

19. If you are going to mix your own formula, you'll need a *pH testing kit*. The easiest type to use is the Colormetric method, such as the Lamotte Soil Testing Kit. This is somewhat expensive; another reason why it is best to use the ready-mix, if only a few bottles are needed.

20. *Transfer case*—a wooden box with glass top and armholes in the front side. (This is not absolutely necessary

and an alternate method of planting without the case is discussed in the section on planting the bottles.)

PROCEDURE

PREPARING THE BOTTLES

1. *Mix the formula;* measure carefully. If the ingredients are not measured carefully, the jelly either will not tell or jells much too hard.

2. *Cook the formula,* bringing to a boil slowly and stirring constantly. Make sure that all ingredients are well dissolved. Watch the Agar especially.

3. While it is still hot, *adjust the pH to 4.8-5.0.* (If you use the ready-mix, you don't have to bother with this step.)

4. *Pour into bottles while still hot.* You will need enough to cover the bottom or side of the bottle about one-half inch to three-fourths inch deep. This means 150 to 200 cc's (⅔ cup) in a 500 cc flask or 200 to 250 cc's (one cup) in the 32-ounce prescription bottle.

5. *Put single-holed stopper loosely in neck of bottle* (stopper must be prepared ahead of time). Stuff the hole about one-half full with non-absorbent cotton packed fairly tight; then dip a small wad of absorbent cotton in Mercurochrome and insert this in the hole of the stopper on top of the non-absorbent cotton. Then pack the remaining part of the hole with non-absorbent cotton. This should be packed tightly enough so that it will not come out easily; yet it should be loose enough to allow some air to filter through. This cotton and Mercurochrome form a trap for fungus that tries to grow through; yet it still allows some air circulation into the bottle.

6. *Cover stopper and neck of bottle with square of cloth, and tie it tightly around the neck with string. Use a bow knot* as hard knots are difficult to untie after being cooked. This cloth keeps the stopper from blowing out of the bottle when it is cooked in the pressure cooker.

7. *Sterilize bottles in the pressure cooker.* Cook for

fifteen to twenty minutes after the cooker reaches a pressure of fifteen pounds. You should also sterilize at the same time all other equipment to be used in the planting process: the medicine dropper, small bottles for washing the seed, small bottles of water for rinsing the seed, et cetera.

8. After cooking, *remove bottles from the cooker immediately. Press down the stopper* as tightly as possible. *Cool the bottles in the position that you want the Agar to jell.* Usually bottles are kept on their sides to give more area for planting your seed.

This is the breaking point in your planting operation. Steps 1 through 8 must be done immediately, one after the other. You can stop now for any length of time, but once you start to plant the seed, you must finish the whole operation at once without stopping.

PLANTING THE BOTTLES   Read over and study all the steps of the planting process carefully until you understand them fully and can do the whole operation without stopping. It is very important to complete the operation without interruption as the entire procedure is based on reducing the chance of infection. You should have all of your equipment ready and be sure of the routine so that the job goes smoothly. The better you know your job and the more quickly you can do it, the better chance of success you will have. Don't be discouraged if your first tries are not successful. Infections happen sometimes even to professionals. After all, we all had to learn in the beginning, and this is a technique which takes practice to perfect.

Prepare and sterilize your planting setup. You will need a place to do the job of planting where you can open the bottles and put in the seed without exposure to fungus in the air. There are two ways to do this:

1. *In the bathroom*—The easiest, cheapest, but poorest way, is to do the job in the bathroom. Put a tray across the washbasin for a work surface. Arrange the bottles to be planted and all other equipment to be used on the tray. Turn on the hot water in the shower or tub as fast as it will go. Then close the door and allow the room to steam well

until moisture condenses and runs down all over the walls and the equipment on the tray. This washes down any fungus which may be on the walls, and the steam in the air settles to the floor as it cools, carrying any fungus present down with it. When the room has been well steamed, remove your outside clothing at least, as it too may carry fungus, and dash into the room to do the planting job. As you can well imagine, this is hot and uncomfortable as you dare not open the windows or even leave the door open until you have finished, but it is a pretty safe way and will usually work all right for a few bottles.

2. *Transfer case*—A safer and better way, especially if you plan to do much bottle planting, is in a transfer case. This is a wooden box with a glass top and armholes with sleeves in the front. It should also have racks across the back to hold as many bottles as possible. You can build your own; it doesn't have to be fancy. The only important thing is that the top should be hinged for easy loading and unloading of bottles and equipment, and it should be as airtight as possible. A transfer case allows you to be outside while only your hands are inside. The small area of the case is easy to sterilize, and being quite airtight, you have a good chance of keeping it sterile throughout the planting process. There is little chance of infection as long as you keep the top closed and do not remove your arms from the case. After all of your equipment is loaded into the case, you should disinfect it thoroughly by spraying with the disinfectant solution. Spray heavily enough to wash down the whole inside of the case and all of the equipment in it. This can be done with the top open. Then you should close the top and spray through one of the armholes thoroughly throughout the case to wash down any fungus spores which may be floating around in the air. Then the case should be used immediately. If you have to stop at any time during the operation and remove your arms from the case, this spraying should be repeated. Transfer cases are used by many people and work very well indeed, but you must be sure to keep all conditions as sterile as possible throughout the whole process.

STEP-BY-STEP PLANTING PROCEDURE

1. *Prepare a solution* of 5 grams of calcium hypochlorite (70% chlorine). Dissolve in 140 cc's of water. Stir the solution thoroughly (it will not dissolve completely). Then filter the solution through laboratory filter paper or several thicknesses of Kleenex through a funnel. (The filter paper or Kleenex should be folded to make a cone which fits the funnel.) To the filtered solution add a few drops of S.T. 37 (a very good disinfecting agent which increases the strength of the disinfecting solution). Also add a few drops of Joy or some other detergent; this breaks the surface tension of the water and allows the seed to get thoroughly soaked, giving a better chance of complete disinfecting. *Warning:* Don't try to keep this disinfecting solution more than a few hours. It should be made fresh every day.

2. *Disinfect the seed.* (Fungus infection can be present in the seed even before planting and must be killed if you are to have any luck at all.) Fill a small two- or three-ounce bottle with glass stopper one-half full of disinfecting solution. Add the seed, then shake hard and long, thoroughly wetting the seed. Seed should stay in solution ten to fifteen minutes. Shake it every two to three minutes. Then place the bottle on its side so that the seed will settle out from the solution. Some types of seed will float to the top; others sink to the bottom. When the seed has separated from the solution, pick the bottle up gently and without shaking it, draw out the stopper, and rotate the bottle slowly as you pour off the sterilizing solution. The seed will stick to the side of the bottle, and you can pour off the solution completely without losing much seed. Immediately refill the seed bottle about one-quarter full with sterile water (which was cooked in small bottles at the same time as the flasks). Shake hard for a minute or two to rinse the seed. If the seed is left in the sterilizing solution too long, it will be killed, as well as the fungus. The bottle must be kept tightly stoppered until used, or the seed can become reinfected.

3. *Disinfect the planting setup and equipment.* Arrange all bottles to be planted, bottles of seed after disinfect-

ing and rinsing, and other equipment, including the Flit gun containing some of the disinfecting solution, and the large bowl containing the balance of the disinfecting solution. Put the medicine droppers in the bowl of solution in the case. Now put on your long rubber gloves. (They will save your hands and arms from being burned by the disinfecting solution. These burns are seldom serious but will make your hands very uncomfortable.) Spray the whole setup well with the solution. Really soak it down so that all surfaces are wet and running with spray. Close the top of the case and spray the air inside until very foggy, using the spray gun through one of the armholes into the case. Now put your arms through the armholes, pulling the sleeves up to the top of your gloves, and dip and wash your gloves in the bowl. Then rinse the medicine droppers in the bowl, squeezing the solution in and out several times.

In the bathroom method this process is the same except that you don't have the case and sleeves and don't have to spray the whole room as the steaming has already washed down the fungus spores in the air.

The preliminaries are over. You are now ready to do the planting.

    4. *Actual planting.* Make sure that you are ready to go —that the bottles to be planted, bottles of seed, medicine droppers, and the bowl of disinfecting solution are within easy reach. From here on out your *success will depend upon the speed with which you operate and your careful attention to directions. Most important thing is to have the bottles open for the least possible time.*

Pull out the stopper; drop it into the bowl.

Take medicine dropper from bowl, open seed bottle, fill with seed and water and

Squirt seed and water from the seed bottle *into the planting bottle.* Three or four squirts per bottle are usually enough. Try to squirt the seed and water over the whole surface of the jelly as evenly as possible.

Put dropper back in the seed bottle *without putting it down anywhere.*

Quickly *put the stopper back in the planted bottles, as tightly as possible,* then gently swish the seed and water over the surface of the jelly to make sure that it is covered evenly. This is important as it spaces the plants more evenly so that they will have more room to grow.

Now you have finished. It is as simple as that. A great deal of preparation for a ten-second job, yet each step is important. There are several small but important points to remember about your movements while planting.

Never put the stopper or medicine dropper down anywhere except in the bottle they came from or in the bowl of disinfecting solution.

Never put your hands and gloves down on the floor of the case or *touch anything except the essential equipment.* If you do touch the sides or floor of the case where the fungus has been washed down and settled, dip your hands in the bowl of disinfecting solution and wash them thoroughly.

Remember, *everything must be sterile.* Fungus grows on Agar even better than orchids. The whole job is wasted if one fungus spore gets in the bottle.

5. *Label each flask* with the name of the cross or the parents of the cross. This may not seem important now, but you'll want to know what your plants are later on.

6. You can repeat step No. 4, the actual planting, as many times as you wish, so long as you do not open the top of the case or remove your arms from the armholes. Once this is done, you must go back to step No. 3 and disinfect the whole setup all over again.

CARE OF FLASKS   After they are planted the bottles should be kept in a place where the temperature is even—somewhere in the 70° to 80° F. range, and they should get about one-third to one-half full sun all day long. Actually, they can do with a great deal less than this, but if you start them off with plenty of sun, the plants will grow hard and strong right from the beginning. It is best to keep the bottles in a fairly humid spot; about 50 per cent humidity is ideal (The jelly in the bottle will dry out if humidity is too low). The seed will start to germinate and show a green any time after ten days, certainly within six weeks from planting.

Infections or contaminations of flasks are usually divided into two classes:

Primary infections, which are the result of contamination at the time of planting and show up within a few days after planting. If your bottles are still clean by the end of the second week, you can be quite sure that they are all right. If primary infections do show up, there is almost nothing that you can do about it; just clean out the bottles and start over.

Secondary infections are the result of fungus which grows through and around the stopper, and they usually do not show up for several months after planting. There are two possible solutions in the case of these secondary infections. Sometimes it is possible to open the bottle and scoop out the small early stage of the fungus infection. If you try this, be sure to scoop out the jelly for some distance around the infection. Then pour a small amount of a fungicide, such as fermate or Natriphene, into the bottle, and gently swish it about for a few minutes; then pour it out and stopper the bottle tightly again. This whole operation should be done in the transfer case under sterile conditions like those used in planting. This works only sometimes and actually is hardly worth the bother. If the plants are large enough, it is better to take them out of the bottle entirely, rinse them in a fungicide, being sure to wash off all the jelly from the roots, and plant them in community pots. This usually works fairly well.

TRANSPLANTING FROM THE FLASK   There are two ways to go about this:

Most people grow their seedlings in the bottles for six to twelve months until they are about one-fourth to one-half inch tall and then transplant to community pots. This is the easiest way, but these small plants are tender, and you may lose quite a few of them before they get accustomed to the brutal conditions of the outside world.

It is safer to transplant the small seedlings back into fresh bottles. Take the young plants out of the original bottle when the first roots begin to show. This is usually when the plants are about one-fourth inch tall, something like three to six months of age. Transplant them into fresh bottles in the sterile transfer case and grow them on until they are three-quarters of an inch to an inch tall. These plants are much stronger and a much larger percentage of them will survive when transplanted to community pots. This is a good deal more work, however, as you must use the same general technique used in planting the seed, and for best results the plants should be spaced carefully in the new flask to give them adequate growing room. One flask or bottle will plant five to ten transplanted flasks or bottles, and as you can imagine, it takes a great deal longer to plant and space these plants individually into the bottles. This means that the bottle stays open longer with a much greater chance of contamination. Your technique must be good to allow you to do this successfully.

COMMUNITY-POT STAGE The community-pot stage is the most ticklish stage of the orchid plant's whole life. The plants are small and tender, and more of them die at this stage than throughout the rest of their lives. These small and tender plants must be handled carefully and gently. Their care must be regular, and the growing conditions must be carefully and consistently maintained.

Planting the Community Pots Step by Step:

1. *Take the plants out of the bottle.* A knife blade or a wire with a hook on the end will do to scoop the plants out of the bottle. Try to scoop the jelly rather than the plants themselves, as bruises at this stage are usually fatal.

2. *Wash the plants in a mild fungicide.* Natriphene works well for this. Be sure to wash off all jelly on the roots and the plant itself because this jelly will attract fungus which can kill the young plants.

3. *Sort plants as to size.* Throw away the smallest plants as they will always be the smallest and slowest growing, taking longer to bloom than the larger ones. It is hardly worth while fooling with plants much less than half an inch tall because the conditions of the outside world are likely to be too harsh for them.

4. *Prepare the pots.* Most people use small pots about

three inches in diameter. Fill the pot about half full of
broken pot, charcoal or small gravel, then fill the pot to the
rim with pine bark. It is best to do this in two layers. Fill the
pot up to about one half inch from the top with coarse or
medium-sized bark. Then fill the top half inch with fine
screenings of bark. It is much easier to plant the seedlings in
this fine bark and it will stay more evenly damp than will the
coarser grades of bark. As the seedlings grow larger their roots
will penetrate to the coarser bark below and do well in it. If
the whole pot is filled with the fine screenings drainage is not
good and the seedlings will not thrive. At this point many
growers either soak the pot, bark and all in a fungicide solution for several hours, or sterilize the pots, bark and all in a
pressure cooker for fifteen minutes at fifteen pounds pressure.
This is more work, but it is a good idea as it rids the pot and
pine bark of the fungus which is almost certainly present in
it, and it gives the plants a carefree and clean start.

5. *Place the plants in the bark.* The easiest way is to use
a pencil or other round and pointed instrument. Make a hole
in the bark large enough to drop in the roots of the plant. Be
careful not to bury its leaves in the bark. The joint where the
leaves meet the roots should be kept at the surface of the bark
with the roots down in the bark and the leaves above. Then
with your pointed instrument push the bark back around the
roots until the plant is held tightly. Repeat this process, adding more plants about one-half inch to three-fourths of an
inch apart until the pot is full. A 3-inch pot will hold from
twenty to forty plants, depending on the spacing.

Due to the ease of handling and the over-all evenness of
growing conditions in community pots of bark, many growers
are using larger pots of shallow depth, like bulb pans, instead
of the small community pots. Some growers even use seedling
flats like those used for annuals, but of course with pine bark
rather than soil. The larger the pot or flat, the more easy it is
to maintain a steady dampness without being too wet one
minute and too dry the next. Under even conditions, the
seedlings grow better and faster than was ever before believed
possible.

6. *Label each pot* with the name of the cross or its parentage.

CARE OF COMMUNITIES   Care of communities is very simple. They want much the same as mature plants in every respect, but the care must be much more regular and constant.

1. *Sun.* At first communities should be given the same amount of light as the plants received when they were in the bottles. Once the plants become well established and rooted into the bark, it is safe to gradually increase the light until the communities are receiving the same amount of sun as mature plants.

2. *Water.* The bark in community pots should be kept *just barely damp* all of the time. A light sprinkling in the

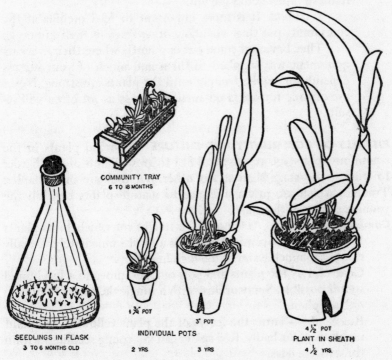

COMMUNITY TRAY
6 TO 18 MONTHS

1 ¾ POT

3" POT

4 ½ POT
PLANT IN SHEATH
4 ½ YRS.

SEEDLINGS IN FLASK
3 TO 6 MONTHS OLD

INDIVIDUAL POTS
2 YRS   3 YRS

26. STAGES OF GROWTH, FLASK TO SHEATH.

morning every sunny day should be sufficient. It is important to water only in the morning. Don't allow the leaves of these young plants to stay wet overnight or "damp-off" (fungus rot) will probably be the result.

3. Young seedlings want *steady humidity*—50 to 70 per cent. Avoid very dry conditions but also avoid very humid and drippy conditions or "damp-off" will almost certainly sweep through the pot almost overnight.

4. *Temperatures* too should be steady. 65° to 80° F. are best as these smaller plants cannot stand extremes of temperatures. If you are growing any quantity of seedlings it will pay to keep the community pots on a bench or tray of gravel with a thermostatically controlled soil-heating cable buried in the gravel. This will keep the pots at an even temperature and result in much better growth.

5. *Food.* It is more important to feed orchids at the community-pot stage than any other stage in their life cycle.

They have just come out of a bottle where their every requirement was supplied to them and much of your success depends on regular feeding until the plants are strong. Never use organic fertilizers on small seedlings as rot often will result.

PITFALLS OF COMMUNITY-POT CULTURE   Orchid plants in the community-pot stage are easy and fast to grow. Plants are no harder to grow at this stage than at any other, but they are more tender. Troubles which are just a nuisance to mature plants can kill the young seedlings at this stage.

Common Troubles   *"Damp-off,"* a fungus rot which turns plants brown or black overnight and kills almost immediately. Usually due to too much water or too high humidity.

Control: Dry the plants and pots out, and move to a less humid spot if possible. Spray or dust with a fungicide, such as Fermate or Natriphene.

Red Spider—Turns the leaves of the plant yellowish and plant usually withers badly. Red spider can kill young seedlings within three to five days.

Control: Dust with flowers of sulphur or better—spray with a miticide, such as Dimite or Kelthane.

Slugs—Slugs come at night, simply move across the pot, mowing down plants like a lawn mower, cutting them right down to the surface of the bark and leaving only roots.

Control: Hand pick them or dust or spray with Metaldehyde; You can also use slug baits. (This is easiest but least effective way.)

TRANSPLANTING FROM COMMUNITY TO INDIVIDUAL POTS   By the time the plants reach a height of two to four inches, they will have become very crowded in the pot and they should then be transplanted to individual pots, or into larger community pots or seedling flats. Seedlings should now be spaced about 3 to 4 inches apart to allow for plenty of growing room. Seedlings can be grown up to blooming size this way and with the new barks it is easier and faster to do so than it is in small individual pots. Many growers transplant into 1¾-inch or 2½-inch pots, but we never use less than a 3-inch pot. When we pot them, we follow methods outlined in Chapter 7. These small plants must be fed heavily and regularly for best results. Seedlings grow rapidly and can often be bloomed in this first pot before needing repotting.

CARE OF SEEDLINGS IN INDIVIDUAL POTS   By the time the plants reach individual-pot size, they can be treated in the same manner as the mature plants, but it is best to make sure that the care is steady and regular. After all, these plants are smaller than mature plants and cannot stand as much abuse and neglect as a mature plant will take.

Careful observation of the plants and their growing conditions is still of utmost importance at all times. By feeding regularly and maintaining good growing conditions constantly, it is quite easy to bloom many seedlings by the time they are four years old. We often bloom seedlings before they are 3½ years old at the Orchid Jungle, and our average is something like 4½ years from seed to first bloom. This may seem like quite a wait, but when you consider that it used to take eight or more years to bloom the plants from seed, it is actually not very long.

Be patient.

It will be well worth it.

Blooming a seedling that you have grown from seed is the ultimate triumph of the orchid grower.

chapter 12

Orchid Corsages and Arrangements

Most beginners prefer to keep their flowers on the plants, but as your collection grows, the temptation to wear your own flowers or use them in flower arrangements will increase. Imagine your satisfaction when friends comment on a corsage or arrangement, and you can answer, "Oh, yes, I grew it myself!"

Florists tend to crowd and overdress flowers so that the ribbons and accessories show more than the flowers. Most orchid growers feel that the flower itself is an individual, that actually this individuality is their special charm.

Making flower arrangements and corsages is a true art, and we do not have room in this book to attempt any real instruction in this field. There are a few suggestions listed below, however, which may help you in your use of orchids in corsages and arrangements:

1. Keep it simple. Don't crowd or overdress the flowers. Depend on the individual flowers and the line and balance of the design for beauty.

2. Use unusual types of orchids for effect.

3. Use in odd numbers, always 1-3-5-7, et cetera.

4. Arrange the flowers in curves to suggest movement or to follow the line of a dress or background of an arrangement.

5. Have a center of interest and work out from it so that the eye is drawn into the center of the arrangement.

6. Design for balance—line, color and mass; all contribute to the balance of an arrangement.

7. Orchid flowers look better right side up. This is usually the only way that you can see into the lip and appreciate the whole beauty of the flower. The flower in the center of interest at least should be right side up. Those out toward the edges may be twisted and turned for effect.

8. For wearing:

Large flowers are dressy (usually should be worn single).

Single flowers of medium size can be casually worn on play clothes, in the hair, et cetera.

Single flowers of the smaller sizes make wonderful boutonnieres for men.

Many of the unusual types of orchids look very sporty.

Sprays of medium to small flowers often look best when worn as they are on their own stem without wiring or ribbon, as they are usually evenly spaced and well held.

9. When combining with ribbons or other accessories, remember these accessories are used to set off the flower and carry out the design, not for their own beauty and certainly not to cover the flowers. Colors of accessories should either match or contrast.

PREPARING FLOWERS FOR CUT WORK:

1. Don't cut until full open, usually two to four days.

2. Cut with a sharp blade. Scissors or clippers bruise the stem so that it cannot pick up water.

3. Put cut stem in water immediately. Use a small-necked container so that the flower itself is supported by the sides and is not actually in the water.

4. Cool in the bottom of the refrigerator. (The vegetable section is best.) Cool for two to three hours at least; overnight is even better. This sets and hardens the flower so that it will hold up better when used.

CORSAGES—MATERIALS NEEDED   Light florist wire, Flora-tape (an adhesive waterproof tape for wrapping flower stems), ribbon and corsage pins are the essentials. Various colored pipe cleaners and netting or lace, small water tubes or flower holders (such as Aquapins, which keep the flower stem in water even when worn so that flowers last better) are also sometimes used.

MAKING THE CORSAGE STEP BY STEP—SINGLE FLOWERS

1. *Tape the stem.* Hold the flower stem in your left hand just behind the flower. Start the Flora-tape at the top

of the stem, spiral downwards, twirling the flower and over-lapping the tape. A light, steady pull on the tape stretches it so that it holds tightly.

2. *Wire the stem.* Hold the wire against the stem of the flower with end sticking out about one-half inch below the end of the stem. Hold flower stem and wire just under the flower with your left hand and wind the long end of the wire two or three turns around the stem just below the flower; then spiral down the stem, finishing up by twisting together the short and long ends of wire to form a long wire tail below the stem.

3. *Cover stem and wire with Flora-tape,* same method as No. 1.

4. *Gently bend flower stem* as close as possible behind

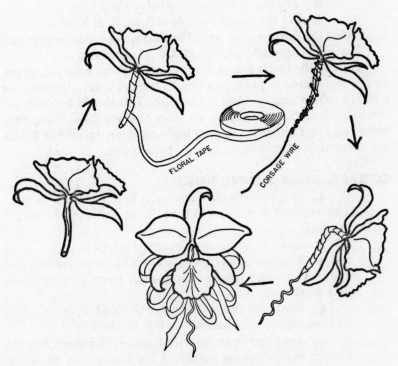

FLORAL TAPE

CORSAGE WIRE

27. STEP BY STEP CORSAGES.

the flower until the flower lies more or less flat against the stem. This bending should be done carefully and gradually without breaking the stem.

5. *Curl the wire tail* around a pencil or pen to make a spiral, or in a flat snail-like curl.

6. *Fix the ribbon bow*. Keep it simple. Two or three bows not wider than the flower are usually enough. Cut off the ribbon ends slightly longer than the bow and on an angle. Tie the bow tightly with florist wire, and use the tail ends of the wire to wire the bow into place. The bow is usually attached at the bend of the flower stem so that it is underneath the flower and supplies a background for it. Tape the ends of the bow wire to the flower stem. This holds the bow steady and keeps it from snagging your dress.

7. *The bow is always worn below the flower.*

8. *Pin the flower on right side up.* This is the only way that the flower shows well. Pin through the tape or over the stem, not through the stem as this causes wilting.

To keep the flower longer in a corsage, you can wrap the flower stem in wet cotton or put it in a slender tube of water, Aqua-pin, or a child's rubber balloon filled with water. This should be done before step No. 1. Then tape and wire over to cover it up. This often looks bulky and actually is seldom really necessary unless the flower is a particularly delicate type, such as Phalaenopsis.

CORSAGES USING SEVERAL FLOWERS

1. Prepare individual flowers as in steps Nos. 1 through 4 above. Each flower should have the long wire tail for wiring together.

2. Use odd numbers of flowers: 1-3-5-7, etc.

3. Design should have: a center of interest, balance and a shape for some special effect—tiara, curve of dress neck, over the shoulder, et cetera.

4. Start with the central flower and add others, winding and weaving the wired stems together for stability.

5. Avoid heavy or crowded bunches of flowers. Arrange so that the individual beauty of the flowers can be appreciated.

6. Once your design is achieved and the tails have been woven together sufficiently to keep the flowers in place, the tail ends can then either be cut off or curled and used to help the design.

7. Ribbons are seldom used with corsages of several flowers. If they are, they should be simple and usually small. They should be toward the bottom center of the corsage, and it is often effective to have longer tails on the ribbon bow so that they hang down below the corsage.

ORCHID ARRANGEMENTS   Making your own arrangements with your home-grown orchids can be a lot of fun, and it will bring extra beauty into your home. Arranging flowers is an artistic expression that anyone can develop. It's easy and a source of never-ending satisfaction. Most people think of arrangements only for special occasions but they should really be for everyday living. Flowers here and there around the house will add much charm and loveliness to any home.

You too, can learn to decorate with flowers. The basic elements are simple and easy:

1. *Location* of the arrangement should be decided on first. Then the arrangement should be designed to fit into, compliment, or contrast with the surroundings.

2. *Proportion* of flowers to container is important. In general, the tallest point of arrangement should be 1½ to 2 times as high as the heighth of the vase or widest part of the bowl.

3. *Balance* is also important. Your arrangement should not look "lop-sided," but balance can be achieved with off-center arrangements as well as symmetrical ones. Oftentimes an off-center balance is more effective and eye-catching than a perfectly centered one.

4. *Contrast* of texture, shape and color make your arrangement more dramatic and interesting. The contrast serves to set each off against the other. Avoid over-all sameness.

5. *Unity* of materials must also be considered. True harmony is the result when flowers, plant materials, con-

tainers and accessories and their location or background seem
to belong together.

DESIGN   There are only a few basic shapes for all flower arranging. Which shape is best depends on several things: Where it will
be used, what flowers you have to work with, the containers available, both as to size and shape.

Triangles can be varied to fit many situations. They can be tall
or wide, they can be symmetrical, with the tallest point in the
middle, or they can be used as right angle triangles with a straight
vertical edge on either side. Low, shallow bowls usually look best
with triangular arrangements. The largest flowers should be used in
the lower, central part of the triangle.

Circles, Crescents and Simple Curves are lovely and natural
forms that lend themselves well to arrangements. Very often the
line or basic shape can be established with plant material and only
a few flowers are needed to complete the arrangement. Usually low
or relatively wide-mouth containers are best for these.

Sword-shaped, tall and slender arrangements, featuring a
straight vertical line can be very effective in corners or narrow
spaces. Tall and small-mouthed containers with stiff and clean-cut
foliage supply the height. Only a few flowers reaching upward along
lower third of the foliage are necessary.

The "S" Curve, often called "Hogarth's Curve" or "the line of
beauty," is another basic design, particularly well suited to tall,
slender containers, particularly urns, bottles and pitchers that have
a definite curving line of their own. The "S" can be achieved with
spray orchids or with plant material with most of the flowers worked
in gracefully through the middle section of the curve.

THREE BASIC STYLES IN FLOWER ARRANGING

Old Fashioned Bouquets or "Traditional" arrangements depend
in large part on quantity and mass of flowers and for this reason do
not lend themselves particularly well to orchid arranging.

Oriental arrangements depend on simplicity and beauty of line;
an elegant and lovely style that sets off a few individual orchid
flowers to best advantage and allows the eye to appreciate the
character of each flower.

Modern arrangements are also very well suited for use with orchids. Like the Oriental, they depend on simplicity of line and the form, texture and color of individual flowers and foliage or plant materials rather than mass effects. Thus the best qualities of orchids can be featured. Though the general effect is often quite Oriental in flavor, Modern arrangements are much less formal and permit the arranger a much wider choice of materials and more originality in design.

There are many fine books on the art of flower arranging available from your local library and bookstore. A little study and practice will soon lead to confidence and ease in flower arranging and many hours of additional pleasure from your orchids. Whatever the décor of your home, you will find you can co-ordinate the color schemes of flowers and furnishings. Use your arrangements as accents in your general decorating. Often the perfection of one flower, artfully displayed, is equally effective as a large and fancy arrangement.

Simplicity is a virtue, particularly when arranging orchids and you will soon find that most arrangements take only a few minutes to design and execute.

Orchids are proud and elegant, yet so extremely versatile that the possibilities for arranging them are sure to stimulate your imagination.

Originality should be your goal.

Try orchid arranging and reap the double rewards of artistic creation and personal satisfaction.

Orchids For Gracious Living!

Common Questions About Orchids

Are there any black orchids?

No! As a matter of fact there is no such thing as a truly black flower of any sort. However, any extra dark flower is liable to be called "black." All of the so-called black flowers; orchids, roses, tulips, anthuriums, etc. are really only dark, dull shades of purple, brown, maroon and combinations of these colors. A few orchids do come with extremely dark spots or stripes that appear almost black, but the main background color is usually green or some other color. The two orchids most often referred to as "black orchids" are: *Epidendrum cochleatum* which has chartreuse sepals and petals with a dark, dull purple lip that appears black from a distance and *Coelogyne pandurata* which has pale green sepals and petals with a greenish yellow lip boldly marked with broad brownish-black veins, ending in a large triangular blackish blotch. Both of these are smallish flowers. If you ever see a large corsage-type orchid that is black, you may be sure that it has been dyed by the florist and is not natural, regardless of the "sales story" that goes with it.

Will enough cold seep through my windows to hurt the plants sitting on the tables and shelves directly in front of the window?

Probably not unless the window is loose in the frame and actually has strong drafts blowing in around it. Storm windows give all the protection your plants need. If you don't have storm windows, you can substitute for them with a thin, clear plastic table cloth from the dime store. Simply tack it or tape it across the window on the inside, from frame to frame. This will insulate your window perfectly and protect the plants very well.

Do I need a wardian case or indoor window greenhouse to grow orchids in my home?

Absolutely not. As a matter of fact, closed glass cases are more likely to harm the plants than they are to help. These cases quickly build up too much humidity, which leads to fungus rot. They also cut down on available light which the plants need. Besides, these cases are expensive and usually an eyesore. Just follow the instructions for the Cake Pan Method of supplying humidity in Chapter 1. Your plants will grow better, with less work for you and you'll have that much more money to spend on your plants instead of on the impractical cases.

Should I spray water on the leaves of my orchids between watering? I have been told to do so twice a day.

This is not necessary and likely to lead to leaf trouble. The Cake Pan Method of supplying humidity described in Chapter 1 supplies all the necessary humidity. If you keep your leaves wet, especially at night, you may soon develop fungus rot in them. If you spray heavily enough for water to run down into the pot, you may also rot off the roots.

Can orchids pick up food or water through the leaves? Does foliage-feeding do any good on orchids?

Most orchid leaves have such a heavy, waxy covering that they cannot pick up anything through the leaves. They have very few stomata, or pores, in the leaf surface and it has never been proven that orchids can pick up any appreciable amount of water or fertilizer through the leaves. It is very doubtful that there is any benefit to foliar feeding.

Will my orchid plants benefit from having a small fan blowing across them?

Perhaps, especially if they are growing in a small area that often becomes stuffy or muggy. Orchids like good ventilation and air movement. A small fan oscillating back and forth across the plants or two or more fans set up to keep the air circulating in a plant room or small greenhouse will definitely prove of benefit. Wind force should be gentle. A light breeze is all that is necessary.

The flower sheath on one of my plants has died and turned brownish black. Another has turned papery and gray. Will they still bloom?

Probably. Many orchids wait several months between making their sheaths and blooming. Often these sheaths dry up in the waiting period, but as their only function is to protect the flower buds from physical damage, they can do so as well when dead as when green and alive. Many orchids regularly bloom through dead and dry sheaths, others often do so. If the normal blooming season goes by without blooms, however, something may have happened to cause abortion of the buds and you will be out of luck until new growths are made and another blooming season comes around.

How long does it take from time flower sheath is produced until flowers appear?

This depends on the individual type of orchid. Some bloom as soon as growth matures. Others bloom while new growth is forming and some wait for several months before flowering. By holding sheath up to the light, you can see the shadow of buds forming. From the time buds are at first visible in the bottom of the sheath to full bloom is usually about 4 to 6 weeks.

Why were my Cattleya flowers smaller this year than they were last year on the same plant?

There could be several reasons for this:

    1.   Plant is not as strong as last year.

    2.   Lack of light. Either dull weather while buds were opening or perhaps you moved it away from the window while the buds were opening. *Buds need light more while opening than at any other time.* If they don't get it, flowers will be smaller, lighter in color and will close up sooner than normal.

    3.   Need of repotting or lack of live roots.

    4.   Lack of fertilizer, or too much nitrogen in the fertilizer.

We do not have much sun during the winter in our part of the country. Do you think we can grow orchids successfully without much sun?

Yes. You should be able to grow and bloom orchids perfectly well in any part of the United States if you have an East, South or West window that gets at least 3 or 4 hours exposure to the sun. Even though the sun is weak and doesn't shine every day, your plants will be able to get by. Just be sure that you give them as much sun as possible during the darker winter months.

Even if you don't have a sunny window, you can grow your plants under artificial light, following suggestions in Chapter 10, and artificial light can also be used to supplement sun in window growing.

One of my plants formed flower buds but they withered and fell off before opening. Why?

Any number of relatively small and unimportant things can happen to cause "bud-drop" without being serious enough to harm the plant. Most likely reasons are: too humid, dark weather; dry windy weather; sudden brief chill or unusually high temperatures; mechanical bruising or injury to buds; moving plant away from sun before buds mature and open.

My plants seem to be growing vigorously and in perfect health but they do not bloom. What am I doing wrong?

Plants that grow well but do not bloom are usually suffering from a slight deficiency of light or food or perhaps a combination of both. If you increase both slightly and maintain on a regular basis, you will probably have blooms on your next new growths.

Does it mean anything when my plants put many of their roots outside the pot instead of down into the potting material?

Most orchids are epiphytes that are used to having their roots exposed to the air. They will often throw some of their roots outside the pot. However, if most of the roots are outside the pot, then your plants probably need repotting, either because the potting material is too old and breaking down, or because you have been overwatering and have turned the potting material sour and caused the roots in the pot to rot.

Are plastic or glazed pots suitable for orchid culture?

It is possible to grow orchids in these pots if you are extremely careful with watering. However, your plants will do better in porous clay pots with less care and constant attention on your part.

How can I tell healthy roots from dead and rotted ones?

Healthy orchid roots are usually white or light gray-green in color. They are firm and turgid to the touch and usually quite stiff. Dead roots are usually brownish-gray and have the crumbly texture of old, wet newspaper. They are very soft and limp and will crumble and fall apart in your fingers.

Is it true that orchids are "Air Plants" and get all of their food from the air without need of fertilizer?

Absolutely not! Orchids are air-plants only to the extent that they do not grow in soil. They still need a well balanced fertilizer just like any other plant. Best results are obtained with inorganic foods of the hydroponic or water soluble type.

Can I use the water from my water-softener for my orchids?

That depends on the type of water-softener you have and the chemicals it uses. Some of these chemicals may be harmful to plants. Others are not. The safest thing to do is write to the manufacturer and ask. He will know.

Do orchids need acidic or alkaline water?

Frankly, it doesn't matter a great deal. Orchids will grow quite well with almost any kind of water. Some experts recommend slightly acidic, others insist on rain water which is almost neutral. Here at the Orchid Jungle we have used fairly alkaline water for over thirty years. Orchids will do well with water in the pH range anywhere from 5.0 (acid) to 8.5 (alkaline) and their range of tolerance may be even wider.

How should you care for deciduous orchids while they are leafless?
Discontinue watering while the plants are dormant. As soon as new growth starts, repot into fresh potting material and resume watering and feeding. Most deciduous orchids want heavy watering and feeding on a regular schedule when in active growth. As growth is completed, start tapering off on frequency and quantity of water and food and stop altogether while leafless.

Do orchids have well defined resting periods or go into dormancy for part of the year?
Some orchids do; others don't. Deciduous orchids have a definite resting period and should not be watered or fed while leafless.
Most monopodial orchids are constantly in growth, though they may grow more actively and rapidly during certain seasons than they do in others. These monopodials want regular watering and feeding the year round.
Most sympodial evergreen orchids grow seasonally and observe a semi-resting period in between spurts of growing. These types CAN be watered and fed slightly more when in active growth than they are in the in-between periods, but actually, they need fairly regular water and food year round. As long as they have live roots, they can pick up and store food for future growth which will be correspondingly stronger.

What are the tiny flea-like insects (gray-green or brownish) that live in the potting material? They come out when I water and they worry me!
They are Collembola or "springtail." They won't hurt your plant at all. They live on dead and decaying matter and have no interest in live plants. Actually, they are feeding on the potting material. Chlorodane powder, of at least 10% strength dusted on the top of the pot and watered in, will control them.

Do the Gibberellins (Gibberellic Acid) have any beneficial effects on orchids?
Not to my knowledge. This chemical has been known and used by scientists for many years in research, but in my opinion has little or

no practical application. It causes individual cells to elongate but usually results in freak growth, tall and weak. After the initial response of tall, quick growth, the effect seems to wear off and you are left with a freak plant that must be nursed back to normal growth. Untreated plants may be left behind during the initial growth response, but within six months will catch up to and surpass the growth of the treated plants, and the untreated ones will be strong, normal plants, much more desirable in every way.

Author's Note: If, after reading this book, you have additional questions about orchids, write to me. I shall be glad to answer them for you to the best of my ability.

T. A. Fennell, Jr.
The Orchid Jungle,
Homestead, Florida.

Glossary

air-plant—common name for epiphytic plants; means that they grow above the ground on trees, cliffs, etc., but do not take food from the tree they grow on—they are not parasites. Actually they don't get food from the air any more than other plants do. They just don't grow in soil.

Aramite—trade name—a miticide that we have used with good results on red spider and other mites, a powder that mixes in water.

back-bulbs—the old bulbs at the back of the plant—ones that are usually cut off and thrown away when large plants are divided, as they are not usually worth growing on—too weak—take too long to flower.

Bi-generic—referring to an orchid hybrid, means a cross of two genera such as Lc or Bc, et cetera.

Black-Rot—usually a fungus infection. See Chapter 8 for description and treatment.

botanicals—all orchids which do not produce flowers of commercial value are usually lumped together into one large group called botanicals, as they are grown for botanical interest—collectors items—only. Considered by many growers to be the most interesting of all orchids.

Cake Pan Method—method of growing orchids in the home; first and only really easy and satisfactory way to grow orchids in the home; now recommended by many growers. It was developed and introduced by the Fennell Orchid Company of Homestead, Florida (*See* Chapter 1).

Captan—a fungicide—new and highly spoken of. Used as a spray, mixed with water.

community pots—pots of seedling orchids which have just been transplanted out of the bottles; the first stage after bottles. The plants are small—½ inch to 1 inch tall and are planted together twenty to forty in a pot. Hence the name "community pot."

Cross-pollination—taking the pollen from one flower and using it to pollinate another flower, resulting in a seed pod and ultimately a hybrid cross; the method of producing new and different orchids.

DDT—trade name for an insecticide that is often used on orchids. When used in an oil-emulsion spray especially formulated for orchids (such as Fenorco Plant Spray manufactured by the Fennell Orchid Company), it is the safest and best all-around spray you can use. It kills almost all insects except red spider and slugs; it is harmless to you unless you are allergic to it.

deciduous plants—plants that drop all of their leaves during one season of the year; in other words, the opposite of evergreen plants.

Dimite—trade name—a miticide made by Sherman-Williams, very good on red spider and other mites but said to be dangerous to humans and pets; use carefully; an oil preparation.

epiphyte—a plant that grows in an elevated position above the ground—on trees or rock cliffs, et cetera, in the wild; commonly called "air plants" to distinguish them from parasites as they do not take food from the tree they grow on; most commonly grown orchids are epiphytes.

eyes—buds which develop into the new bulbs or growths; usually found at the base of mature bulbs at level of rhizome; some types of orchids also have eyes on the upper part of the bulb or stem, which can produce side shoots or new plantlets when the plant is extra strong or when some shock, such as the death of the eyes at the base of the bulbs, forces the others to develop.

Fermate—a fungicide often used on orchids; can be dusted or mixed in water and sprayed directly onto infected areas or cuts.

"Flowers of Sulphur"—a type of sulphur good for dusting as a miticide (but weak)—also used to dust cuts and bruises in plants to keep out fungus infections, a powder available at drugstores.

genus (plural—genera)—the orchid family is divided into many smaller groups of closely related types of orchids. These smaller groups are called the genera; the individual types in each genus are the species. The first word of a botanical name of a plant is the genus name and is always capitalized. The second word is the species name and is not usually capitalized. For example: *Cattleya trianaei*—*Cattleya* is the genus; *trianaei* is the species name.

heating—organic fertilizers if applied too heavily actually give off heat as they decompose or rot. This can kill plant roots and, if it gets too hot, may start rotting in the plant itself.

humidity—water vapor in the air; measured as *relative humidity* which is the percentage of water vapor in the air as compared to the amount of vapor the air could hold. The warmer the air is, the more water it can hold. This explains why the air usually feels drier in the middle of the day than it does morning and evening. The temperature goes up; the water vapor remains the same; but the air could hold much more so the effect is drying. Because of this, watering of plants should be done in the middle of the morning as the day gets warmer. Build up humidity when needed.

hybrid—the result of cross-breeding two different orchids; this produces a new and different orchid which is a hybrid.

hybridization—the act of crossing two different types of orchids to produce a new and different orchid.

hydroponic fertilizer—a special type of fertilizer which is made to be dissolved in water and supplied to the plant just like a regular watering. Fenorco Orchid Plant Food is one of these especially made for orchids by the Fennell Orchid Company, Homestead, Florida.

lead—the growing front of the plant or the new growth or new bulb at the front of the plant; a plant that has branched into several growing fronts is spoken of as a plant with several leads, etc.

Malathon—a fine general insecticide; effective on most garden insects but can also kill animals and people. Take all recommended precautions. Not effective on red spider and slugs.

Metaldehyde—a very effective spray for slugs; poisonous to humans and pets; keep out of their reach. Available from California Spray Chemical Corporation.

miticide—an insecticide or spray that kills mites (red spider). Dimite and Aramite are good ones.

Monopodial plants—means "one foot"; a plant with a single base, such as any common tree; in other words, a plant that grows straight up without branching sideways and growing out across the ground or other growing surface; as opposed to sympodial plants which branch and spread across the ground like the iris or many orchids for instance.

Natriphene—trade name—highly recommended fungicide—powder or tablets—must be kept sealed when stored or takes up water and spoils; good for spraying or dipping.

Natural habitat—the natural or native home or environment of an orchid—the place and climate where an orchid grows wild.

organic fertilizers—fertilizers developed from living sources, such as manure, fish meal, fish-oil emulsions, et cetera. As opposed to inorganic fertilizers which are made up entirely of minerals or chemicals.

osmunda fiber—a coarse black or brownish fiber; the roots of the osmunda fern; found in swampy places all over the United States east of the Rockies; used to pot orchids because it holds some moisture, yet allows good drainage and ventilation so that it does not stay soggy and wet. Lasts two to three years before rotting.

ovary—the stem which runs from the flower to the main flower stem, is actually the ovary which, when pollinated, swells up to form the seed pod and produce the seed.

parasite—a plant that lives on another plant, sending its roots into the other plant to pick up the food which the other plant has prepared for itself, so that it is not necessary to make its own food. Mistletoe is a parasite. Orchids are not. Orchids are epiphytes as they grow on other plants but do not take food from them; they merely sit on them.

Parathion—one of the best general insecticides but can kill animals and people too so should be used carefully. Follow all recommended precautions. Not effective on red spider or slugs.

pH—the measure of acidity or alkalinity of a substance; important in the mixing of orchid Agar-Agar jelly.

pollinia—pellets of pollen; many thousands of pollen grains fused together to form each pellet; number of pellets varies with different types of orchids—2, 4 and 8 per flower.

poly-generic—means several genera—referring to orchid hybrids; a poly-generic hybrid is one resulting from the crossing of several different genera; such as a Blc or Slc x Bc, et cetera.

pseudo-bulbs—the "bulbs" of most types of orchids are correctly called pseudo-bulbs (which means "false bulbs") because, botanically speaking, they are actually only swollen stems which look like bulbs but do not do the true work of a bulb.

red spider—an insect sometimes found on orchids; a type of mite; not actually a spider. (*See* Chapter 8 for description and control.)

rhizome—the connecting stem, between the bulbs or upright growths of an orchid, from which the roots are produced.

rostellum—a damlike growth, between the pollen capsule and the stigmatic surface, on the underside of the sexual column. Keeps the flower from being pollinated by its own pollen.

scale—actually a group of many related kinds of insects; Bois Duval or "white cottony" scale is most common on orchids. (*See* Chapter 8 for description and control.)

semi-terrestrials—orchids that grow just above the ground on the bases of trees, rock outcroppings, et cetera, so that their roots run down into the ground; usually in very light and open, well-drained soils, such as leaf mold or compost.

sheaths—there are two types of sheaths on orchid plants: *Bulb sheaths*—a paperlike covering, which is grayish white and brittle when bulbs are mature; it protects the new growth and strengthens it when young, then dies when bulb becomes mature. *Flower sheaths*—an envelope which grows out of bulb at joint with leaf; protects flower buds as they form; buds grow up and break through in order to bloom; also helps support young and weak flower stem.

slugs—actually snails that do not have shells; often a pest on orchids. (*See* Chapter 8 for description and control.)

species—(this is singular, not plural)—an individual and distinct type of orchid; one that is found growing in the wild. Several distinct or individual, but closely related, species make up a genus. The botanical name of a plant is made up of two names.

The genus name first, capitalized; then the species name which is not usually capitalized. See *genus* for further explanation.

specimen plants—plants of any type orchid which have been grown much larger than usual to provide showy examples of the grower's art and science; the sign of a fine grower.

stigma or **stigmatic surface**—the female organ of the flower; a depression on the underside of the sexual column just behind the pollen cap and rostellum. Usually is filled with a sticky substance to hold the pollen.

substance—referring to orchids means the weight or thickness and strength of the tissue of the sepals, petals and lip of the flower. Heavy substance is desirable as it usually means that the flower is long-lasting.

sympodial plants—those that grow in a creeping fashion, putting up several growths from a common base which spreads sideways across the ground or other growing surface; as opposed to monopodial plants which grow up and ever upwards from a single permanent base.

terrestrial orchids—those that grow in soil like other plants.

transfer case—(See Chapter 11 for description and use.)

Tri-generic—referring to an orchid hybrid; means one resulting from a cross of three genera such as Blc, Slc, Bsc, etc.

viability—the ability to germinate (referring to seed).

virus—a disease of orchid plants. (*See* Chapter 8 for description and treatment.)

Index

No 1 C Daskelliana

No 2 Cattleya Trianae

No 3 C Skinneri

No 4 Lancyp X C Trianae

No 5 L Derrynane C mix palm x2

No 6 C Barbra Billingsley

No 7 C Enid XX ?